1

Paradise (Apparently)
Welcome to Switzerland

Flo Regina

Dear Karen,
Have fun and reflect!!
Flo

Paradise (Apparently) ®

Cover design and illustration by CIRIECO DESIGN
www.knowitall.ch +41 22 774 45 32

Translated and adapted by Julian Plumley and Paul Jarvis (as of the chapter 'Punctuality') from the original Italian version "Un Paradiso Apparente".

First published in Switzerland in August 2009. This edition published in December 2009.

Proofreaders:
Julian Plumley
Paul Jarvis
Lisa Cirieco

Thanks to all those special people I met in Switzerland who inspired me to write Paradise (Apparently).

Thanks to Julian and Lisa; without their encouragement this book would have just stayed on my computer. With their help I was able to accomplish it!

Thanks to my husband, children and to my sister/friend, Serena, who have always supported me.

Paradise (Apparently)
Welcome to Switzerland

The School

The University

At Work

A Survival Guide for Foreigners in Switzerland

Foreword

I was born in Bari, a sunny city in the south of Italy. I lived for 24 years in my native city; for the people of Bari, love, friendship and the family represent the essence of life. Hospitality is sacred and your neighbour is a potential friend whom you can count on. We are social, lively, and cheerful and we always greet each other with hugs and kisses, calling each other 'beautiful' and 'dearest'. I like to point out the good things about my city; I'll let others talk about the bad things.

I have lived in Geneva, Switzerland, for five years in a state of amazement and incredulity, from which I have still not recovered.

I might appear to be a woman, who is rather unreceptive to other cultures, a bourgeois provincial from Bari who only moved to live in a country far away from Italy – or at least far away from my beloved South – at the age of 32. But it's not like that. At 18, I lived for nine months in London; at 20, thanks to the Erasmus programme, I studied for a year in Salamanca, Spain; at 26, I lived for seven years in Brussels and I married a Dutchman at 30. I have lived for years in an international context and I love foreign cultures. My husband is from Amsterdam and I wonder if a bourgeois provincial from Bari would have put up with a partner wearing short white socks under elegant trousers, or bread and cheese for breakfast or the bag of potatoes given to us by a Dutch uncle for our wedding. In short, to be happy after 10 years of marriage it has been fundamental to adopt an approach of absolute openness to other cultures.

Our children are bilingual and bicultural; they speak fluent Italian and Dutch, and are at ease with both of our cultural backgrounds. The habits and customs of the Dutch don't bother me at all any more. When we go to the country of windmills and my mother-in-law goes out cycling with wet hair at five degrees below zero without ever getting a stiff neck; and my children are dressed in hat, scarf and overcoat while their cousins of the same age are dressed in tee shirts and are nourished solely by bread, cheese and potatoes, I don't let it disturb me at all. I remain friendly and calmly accept this cultural diversity.

So the sense of amazement and incredulity that I have lived with for more than five years in Switzerland, and still experience every day cannot be attributed to my lack of cultural flexibility. I think this needs to be said before beginning to recount the tale of the years we have spent in the Swiss Confederation.

My account of life in Switzerland is a bit different from the account of a typical expatriate who only lives for a few years in Geneva, who communicates only in English, who works in an international context, and spends most weekends skiing in the mountains, mixing only with foreign friends. That kind of experience of a foreign country is at times distant from the local realities, from the real local culture and from participation in all the diversity of the host country.

The observations shared in this book are not intended in any way to hurt the feelings of the Swiss. Often, the behaviour, habits and customs that are normal in the host nation can appear bizarre, surprising or unusual in the eyes of foreigners.

The main objective of this book is to let the reader smile at the ironies and the funny side of our experiences in Switzerland. I hope you enjoy Paradise (Apparently)!

Geneva

Our First Day in Switzerland

So there we were; the aircraft was ready to depart and take us to Geneva. Brussels, after my seven years there, had become my home town by adoption. My children didn't have a clue what was going on: Alice was only 3 months old and Dante about two. We were full of hope and ready for a new adventure, convinced we had taken the right decision. We were going to live in a rich country, with a very low unemployment rate, with great opportunities for my husband Harold's career. Life is strange. I had never expected that I would ever live in Geneva… but then I had never expected that one day I would marry a Dutchman!

Harold is blond, a fanatical "Ajax" supporter, talkative, lively and a sleepwalker. He is probably the only certified case of a mummy's boy in Holland. At least I never came across another in the land of windmills and tulips. He is a great sportsman and he sings and plays the guitar – which has been an important aspect of his life as a conqueror of the gentle sex. But I have never understood why Harold gets so stressed out over trivial things. His best friends have told me that I could be the reason – and I'm not excluding any valid hypotheses!

The first time my cousin Alessandra from southern Italy – she has olive-dark skin and is addicted to sunbathing – saw Harold, she asked me:

'Is he an albino?'

I replied:

'No, he's Dutch.'

He doesn't have much hair left, probably because of all that stress. For our wedding photo, my brother's barber had to back-comb his hair!

We got on the plane and I said goodbye to my adoptive city. I had picked Brussels for professional reasons; but Geneva was fate. I had wanted to live in Brussels: the European city, the home of the European institutions. And I had always dreamed about living abroad. A convinced European, I was one of the many lawyers specialised in European Community law who gum up the European Parliament and the workings of the Commission by trying to be the best of Brussels lobbyists. I had many friends who shared my passion and lived in Brussels. In short, that city had become my home and I had worked hard on my career there, sweating blood it seemed.

Another wonderful aspect of my life in Brussels, and one that I had already much appreciated during my time on the Erasmus programme in Spain, were my varied friends: a lovely girlfriend from Alicante – a 31-year-old virgin with her Irish Catholic fiancé; a delightful gay Pakistani friend – a 21-year-old Chemical Engineer; wonderful Dutch and German friends; and my Polish 'eccentric genius' girlfriend who was always looking for a man. I was surrounded by friends from different countries and diverse backgrounds – how wonderful! It was a stimulating and interesting atmosphere. In my home town of Bari, I had always missed this multicultural aspect. Now I was moving to Geneva, an international city and seat of the United Nations, and I was sure that I would not miss this opportunity to move in such an international environment.

The multinational company that Harold worked for had arranged an apartment for six months in Champel, in the centre of Geneva, with a view of the "Jet d'eau" fountain. This was intended to give us time to find a permanent home. We landed at Geneva airport, which was small, clean and well organised. With all our luggage, we joined a queue for a taxi. When our turn came the taxi driver asked us if we had car seats for the children. But given the amount of luggage we had to take, it had been impossible to carry the children's car seats by hand – they were being shipped in one of our two hundred packing cases. I explained to the driver that we did not have the car seats with us while my husband started to load our luggage in the car. The driver rudely told Harold to take the bags out of the car and added:

'I can't take you in my taxi without car seats for the children in case the police stop us, or we have a terrible accident in which one of your children die, or maybe you or your husband die, and I would be in serious trouble.'

He managed to leave out of his list the fact that, in this hypothetical tragedy, he could be as dead as the rest of us! But I have always been chronically superstitious and the accident described by the taxi driver worried me. I tried to touch wood, thinking about the blood-curdling scenario of a fatal accident just described by our kind driver. Meanwhile, my more practical-minded husband, convinced that my worries were completely idiotic, tried to persuade the taxi driver to take us to our apartment. No way – the driver ignored him completely and started loading the next customer in the queue. We waited in the queue for over an hour while driver after driver refused to take us. Alice was crying with hunger and my husband was on the edge of a nervous breakdown. We could have reached the city centre by train, but that would have meant two further bus journeys and a long walk, which would have been hell with all the bags and the two children.

Finally, Mohammed turned up, a friendly Moroccan taxi driver, who had only been in Geneva for a few months. Visibly nervous, with a silent gesture he frantically loaded the taxi. Once inside the vehicle, he whispered that if the police stopped him, he would get a huge fine and might lose his licence. Harold and I, who have always been convinced of the importance of the children's car seats, were struck by the seriousness of the taxi drivers and of the Geneva police. We took this incident to be a point in favour of the Swiss Confederation.

It was seven p.m. when the taxi driver left us in front of the block of flats. The keys for the flat, along with a pile of instructions, had been left there by the agency in charge of our transfer. The building was part of a residential complex of huge, anonymous blocks of flats and it seemed ugly and drab to me, even if it was clean and well organised. We reached the seventh floor and entered a large apartment. It was bleak and unwelcoming, filled with sad old brown furniture. On the walls there were ugly pictures of ravens and ducks, bordered in black. Even with all the lights on, we could not see well, because the bulbs were so dim.

How sad! I am the daughter of an architect and an art dealer, and I had always grown up in houses which were bright, colourful and full of beautiful pictures. But there was no time to feel sorry for myself – I needed to organise dinner. Like a good Italian, I suggested to my husband that I go and fetch some pizza for dinner. Dante wanted to come with me. Harold and Alice remained in the flat while Dante and I went looking for a pizzeria. What luck! Right in front of the ugly complex was a little pizzeria run by a man from Gallipoli – we Apulians are everywhere! A few minutes later I had the boxes in my arms: three pizzas, red-hot and fragrant.

I hurried back to the block so we could eat them while they were still hot. It was just after eight p.m. when we arrived at the doorstep and I realised the door was locked. The key did not open the door. How strange! I tried and tried again, but it was no use. I saw that there was a keypad on the wall by the door. It looked like a cash machine or an alarm system. I had forgotten my cell phone. There was no entry phone. How strange! I managed not to get upset and looked for someone to help me. I saw a man of about 50 looking down nervously from a balcony, and with a big smile, and in my best French – but with a strong Italian accent – I asked for the code to enter. While I waited, with the pizzas burning in one arm and a hungry child on the other, this helpful man went back into his flat and locked his windows. I noticed another lady approaching the door opposite mine and tried to explain the situation, but she did not reply. She ignored me completely, entered the secret code for the door opposite to mine and went in, making sure she closed the door immediately.

I kept calm and forced myself to think positive thoughts about these people, who might well be foreigners themselves and unable to speak French. Then another resident approached the door next to mine and I asked him politely for help in French and in English. Nothing – I was ignored again. The pizzas were cold. We had been there for over an hour, Dante was crying and I was really beginning to lose patience. I rushed to block the way of a lady who was entering the block and asked her in a loud voice to let me in. She replied:

'I don't know you, you could be a thief, I'm not going to give you the code, and if you really lived here you would know the entry code yourself.'

And so for the umpteenth time the door was slammed in my face. I have honestly never seen a thief with pizzas in one hand and a hungry two-year-old in the other. I was astonished, speechless and out of ideas. I must have had my typical gormless expression on my face. At half past nine, I started to shout for Harold and he appeared a few minutes later together with a few of the other tenants and said: 'Did you go to Bari to get the pizzas? What have you been doing? Come up so the pizzas don't get cold. Didn't you have the key?'

He opened the door with Alice in his arms. I told him what had happened. With the cold pizzas in our stomachs, we went to bed exhausted, with thoughts of our welcome to Switzerland still fresh in our minds.

Brussels, Five Months Earlier...

I was expecting Alice, and Dante was only 18-months-old. One evening Harold said to me over dinner:

'There are some great opportunities for my career in Geneva or London, would you like to change country?'

I clearly remember that cold and rainy April evening, it was much like every day in Brussels, where the sun rarely shows its face. I had worked all day, eight months pregnant and weighed down by 25 extra kilos; my feet had turned into rugby balls. My shoe size had gone from 38 to 40. Harold called me the 'untransportable lady'; maybe I should have been in the Guinness book of records for the most weight put on during a pregnancy. I had broken a bed, destroyed a sofa and I could no longer fit in a cinema seat. On top of that, I had constant nausea.

I felt disgusting. I had always been quite slim and to see myself in that state was no fun at all. And if that wasn't enough, I was in charge of the legal department of a banking consortium, a very stressful job. And once I got home, I obviously had to look after Dante who had suffered from insomnia since his birth. All in all, I was exhausted.

'Harold, you know that I love Brussels, I have been here for many years and I have lots of friends here, I have a great job and I feel at home. And we bought this apartment; it doesn't seem like a good idea to start again from zero.'

My husband tried to change my mind, adding:

'We will have places at an international school paid for by the company. Remember we are talking about London and Geneva – both are great cities. And Geneva is small, liveable and very international, just like Brussels. I would get a big pay raise and you could take a break from work. You could spend more time with the children and then, when you wanted to, look for another job. There are lots of job opportunities in either city.'

He had pressed the right buttons: my desire to take a career break, to stop work and be able to rest. In fact, I had devoted all my time and energy to my career and not had time to do anything else. London frightened me, too big and spread out: to go and see friends would be too complicated because of the distances involved. I thought about it and I reasoned that Geneva, where I had spent a lovely weekend several years before, was a small, very liveable and international city. And on top of that we would have an exclusive school for the children, all paid for... not bad! A break from work would do me a lot of good. Harold's proposal began to seem attractive.

'Yes, we could move to Geneva, but I wouldn't want London. Geneva is clean and structured. And thanks to all the international people there, it could be the ideal location for us. And everyone knows Switzerland is a very well-run and modern country.'

And in the end, we made our big decision.

I announced the news to my parents and they said to me:

'You couldn't have made a better choice. Geneva is a marvellous city. Spotless, efficient, and well-organised. We have been to Switzerland lots of times and it is one of our favourite places to go on vacation. We're really happy for you both and above all, the children will be very happy there.'

A Desperate Housewife

And so began our new life in Geneva. I was enthusiastic. When I woke up in the morning, after a broken night's sleep due to the children, the sun was shining. This might seem a rather banal comment. But for a Barese who had lived seven years in Brussels, where the sun shines for maybe fifteen days a year, it was an indescribable pleasure. Besides, our apartment was very close to Lake Léman, it was still summer, and the spotless beaches of Geneva were still open and full of people. Everything was beautiful, the mountains, the sun, the lake, the absolute cleanliness and order. It seemed to me to be a magical place. My mother, who had come to the rescue to help me with the children, ventured to draw my attention to the fact that the city seemed to be a pretty expensive place. One day she had returned from the bakery in a state of shock after paying fifteen Swiss Francs for a kilo of bread. I didn't pay any attention to what she was saying; I didn't want to listen to any negative comments on my paradise on earth.

But I quickly realised that I was not on holiday, but rather in forced labour. Harold left home early in the morning and left me with the children. I didn't even know where the supermarket was, the playgrounds, a paediatrician or a pharmacy. I have always had the knack of being able to chat to all sorts of people – the porter, the neighbours, the baker – which is how I organised the family's basic needs within the span of a few days. The work was endless. I didn't have anyone to help me, no babysitter and no one to help with cleaning.

My two tiny children filled my entire day. I couldn't get a full night's sleep; Alice woke every two hours. And whenever she was asleep, Dante would be crying out with night-terrors. It seemed that I hadn't quit work, but rather I was working 24 hours a day on a huge and infinite job. Only those who have found themselves having to look after two small children with only a year's difference in age will understand what this is like. I had never been as tired in my whole life. Working in an office seemed like a walk in the park compared to the enormous effort of raising two children, practically on your own, in a foreign country.

My typical day, after a terrible night, would start with attempting to wash and dress the children and settle them into their 2-seater pushchair to reach the Parc Bertrand. The journey wasn't easy. On some short stretches I had to ask for help to lift the enormous buggy and I rarely found anyone willing to help me. I was exhausted, neglected, badly dressed, overweight, alone and desperately pushing my little angels. At the park, I was often mistaken for a babysitter or even for an au pair girl. Not only because of my appearance, but also because my children are blond like their father while I have a distinct Mediterranean look.

After two months of this life I decided to threaten my husband:
'Either you pay for a babysitter or within 24 hours you are going to be paying the same money for a psychologist!'

Harold was worried about the high cost of living in Switzerland and I was a hair's breadth away from a nervous breakdown. The Dutch are well known for being tight with money, but my threats were effective. A week later, Fanny, a splendid Paraguayan girl, was helping me for several hours a day. What a difference in my life! I could finally take a shower with the door closed, I had time to straighten my hair with a hairdryer and I could even have a phone conversation!

I quickly realised there were big advantages to living in Switzerland:
- Cleanliness and good organisation
- Excellent quality of life
- A clear lake with lots of spotless beaches
- An exceptional health system
- Quality schools

- A complete absence of queues, even at the supermarket

In short, it seemed to us that we were in a paradise and we did not regret our decision to move to Geneva.

My new neighbour on the seventh floor, Mme Emilie, was always kind and asked me if everything was going well. One day I met her husband, a retired bank official, in the lift. I attempted to break the ice by asking if there had been any cases of burglary in the apartment block.

He replied intolerantly:

'Madame, there are no Swiss thieves. It's only the Italians or French that cross the borders to come and rob our homes.'

The Tram

One day, feeling well-rested thanks to Fanny, I decided to go and visit an Italian friend with kids the same age as mine. So I ventured out to the tram, full of enthusiasm, with the infamous 2-seater pushchair. It was a beautiful day and it was good to be getting to know people. I am not a solitary sort of person and I love having company. The tram arrived punctually at the stop. A man pushed the button and the door opened automatically. But while I was trying to haul the pushchair inside, I realised I had chosen the wrong door. For someone newly arrived in the city that was completely understandable... in the extremely organised and immaculately clean Genevan public transport system there is a door specially designed for entering with strollers. But I hadn't known that.

While I was pushing and trying to get onto the tram, the tram driver was getting irritated at the delay and decided to close the doors, leaving me on the pavement. The pushchair remained jammed between the automatic doors. I started to panic. The children were in danger of being squashed, and I started to call for help from the stunned passengers, who were watching the tragedy unfold from their comfortable seats and making no effort to help. The driver started to drive off, he hadn't noticed anything. I shouted, but no one helped me. I started to use some colourful phrases in my Barese dialect. (In cases like this it is really inevitable, given the seriousness of to the situation.) No one helped me at all. Finally the imbecile driver noticed my shouts and opened the doors. I got down and freed the pushchair from the jaws of the door. The children were thankfully unhurt; they were simply looking at me curiously wondering why mummy had been screaming so much. I tried to get back on using the right door, but the driver had already closed it, leaving me stranded.

We didn't have a car so we decided to rent one for a month before buying one. I took Alice to look for a paediatrician since she had a high fever and I have always been a terrible hypochondriac when it comes to me, let alone my children. The doctor's office was five minutes away from our home by car. Unfortunately, I have no sense of direction and I was still not familiar with the layout of the streets. Even after living for twenty four years in Bari I still continue to get lost and have trouble finding my friends' houses. Imagine me trying to get around Geneva after only two months!

I looked for help, but I couldn't find anyone willing to give me directions. Alice was burning hot and she was crying in the car. Finally, I arrived at the paediatrician's office, but I couldn't find a parking place. I phoned the doctor's secretary to tell her I would be ten minutes late. This bureaucrat replied in a dry tone:

'If you don't arrive with your child within two minutes, the doctor will no longer have time to see you.'

Worried, I reassured her:

'I am already right in front of your door, I will park and I'll be there right away.'

After a couple of times driving around the block I still couldn't find a parking space. Finally I saw a place that was about to become free, but to get to it quickly I would have to reverse down a one-way street. I decided to reverse down the street, a distance of 50 metres. While I was concentrating on the task of reaching the empty space, an old and slight man walked into the centre of the street, forcing me to brake quickly to avoid hitting him. I thought he was trying to help me, I smiled and thanked him. I saw that he was waving his hands but I couldn't hear what he was saying to me. I looked again in the mirror and noticed that he was deliberately blocking my way. Was this kind gentleman trying to tell me that I was about to knock into something without realising? I lifted the hand brake, got out of the car and said:

'Thank you for your help, am I making a bad manoeuvre?'

'You are reversing the wrong way down the street, and I will not let you pass. You need to go around the block and drive the right way up the street.'

I looked carefully at this man; he must have been 70-years-old, dressed in a dated blue jacket and with an unbearable expression on his face. I was in a hurry. I had no time to argue and I repressed the desire to slap him. I am not a violent person and I had never had such an instinct in the past, such a strong desire to do violence. I went back to the car, went around the block again but when I returned, the parking space was no longer there. I wanted to cry and to scream!

After a while I eventually found a space. I arrived at the paediatrician's office and the secretary announced I was too late. I explained that I couldn't find a parking space and pleaded with her to take Alice as an emergency. My face was desperate, I was distressed and I think that I actually moved the doctor's secretary to compassion. An hour later the paediatrician examined Alice. Fortunately, since she ended up in hospital as a result. In a few weeks my daughter's health was restored. I must say the hospitals are exceptional, the doctors efficient and the organisation impeccable. I felt I was in a five star hotel.

House Hunting

The stress and the difficulty of finding a house, and of registering Dante at a nursery, increased my state of nervousness. The company where my husband works, 'Cleancorp', had arranged for us to stay in the rental apartment for only a few months, after which we would have to vacate it for other families arriving in Geneva. Cleancorp were generously paying the rent for our apartment for that short period. My husband and I had no idea of the cost of renting apartments in Geneva. At the estate agent's we discovered that we were living in one of the most exclusive parts of the city. To think it had seemed to be an ordinary apartment block. The rent for our apartment was 10,000 Swiss Francs per month! That was well out of our budget, without a shadow of a doubt. A typical mortgage to buy a house would certainly cost less; it was better to invest in Swiss bricks and mortar.

Our wish was to buy a villa and since my husband was working all day it was up to me to look for a house. I thought if I worked on it full time, I would manage to find one in a short time. But I had not taken into consideration the following facts:

Firstly, I was alone with two small children. Secondly, we still hadn't bought a car and we had to give the rental car back as the cost was too high. Thirdly, Geneva had a huge housing shortage – not enough houses for the number of residents. In 2003, the year in which we moved to Geneva, the housing boom was at its peak. It was a real lottery to find an apartment or a villa to rent or to buy. Impossible to find a house! An unimaginable situation. In the newspapers, houses for sale were few and far between and too expensive. Only one villa every three weeks would fit our budget.

At Cleancorp, the number of employees had grown excessively in no time, from 300 to 2,000 employees, and all these newly-arrived families were looking for a place to live. It was a ferocious battle as the number of offers diminished and the prices went up. In truth, Cleancorp had contributed significantly to the dire housing situation in Geneva. It had been difficult before, but now it was simply impossible.

Time was passing quickly and our rental contract was about to expire. We had asked to prolong the contract, even though we hated the sad and noisy apartment. On the floor above lived a family with four small children who woke up crying every morning at about 6 a.m. But we had no other choice, in fact we were lucky to have a roof over our heads, given the situation.

Getting to view the houses was a battle, a dogfight. As soon as the adverts were published in the newspaper, I quickly made appointments with the agencies, who I attempted to move to pity with the story of our difficulties and the urgent need we had to buy a house. They never did take pity and what's more they would never call us back if I didn't chase them down. A nightmare! I would arrive at a villa and there would already be a queue of people interested in buying it, lots of them colleagues of Harold. Often on a Monday, I would make an arrangement to see a villa three days later, only to be told on Tuesday that the house was already sold.

Among the few buildings that we managed to see was a small but beautiful villa a few kilometres from Geneva. I immediately fell in love with that villa. We were among many people visiting the villa at the same time and I tried to suck up to the lady from the agency. Harold was enthusiastic, so we informed her that we were seriously interested.

The imperturbable estate agent told us:

'You are not the only ones; there are a lot of families interested in buying this villa. Fill in the standard form to make an offer, and then the owner will make the decision.'

Perfect, I thought. We would fill in the form and offer the exact amount asked for in the advert. We were convinced that since we hadn't tried to lower the price by even 50 Swiss Francs, the house would be sold to us. That week was long. We fantasised about our imminent move into the beautiful villa. The telephone rang seven days later and the lady from the agency stated:

'I am sorry, Madame, but your offer was not accepted. The owner preferred to sell to another family.'

'I'm sorry but I don't understand. Did they offer more than us or are they friends of the vendor?'

'Absolutely not. They offered exactly the same as you, but they had more in cash. Since we are not in Italy here, personal recommendations don't work.'

'I'm sorry, what do you mean? We also had part of the total in cash but no one asked us for this information. We are really interested in buying the house and we are prepared to offer more than the asking price, if necessary.'

In reality, I was lying, because we couldn't have offered any more. But, as a good Italian, I wanted to understand if they had sold to a family member or to someone who had been recommended to them.

Very irritated at my insistence and all the questions, she replied:

'I don't have time to discuss this further; the villa has been sold to someone else and it's useless to talk further about it. Good day.'

Disillusioned and glum, we continued with our search.

We then got an appointment to see a villa outside our budget, but we were desperate and ready to try anything. At the end of the visit, we said to the Belgian lady from the agency:

'We like the house a lot but it may be a bit too expensive.'

She didn't seem bothered and in fact, she smiled and said:

'If you have cash I can lower the price without a problem.'

'I'm sorry, I don't follow. Could you clarify that?'

'If you pay a part of the house under the counter, we can lower the price.'

We could not have afforded the house, it was too expensive, and we didn't want to pay a part under the counter, risking legal problems in our new host country. But I couldn't believe it... if you mix up paper and plastic in the rubbish and fail to recycle them you get a letter from the court, and if you make any noise after 10 p.m. the police arrive. But this estate agent was trying to sell a villa illegally? No, it wasn't possible. I couldn't believe it.

I became a sleuth of estate agencies; I knew all the agents. So much so that to avoid dealing with me they would tell their secretaries to deny they were there. I was intolerable, probably transmitting to the estate agents all of my anxiety about the search for a house. By then I was getting insistent and aggressive. But after all, the agents considered us to be beggars, and Switzerland does not belong to the poor, and certainly not to unfortunate wretches pretending to be able to buy a house. This depressed me a lot, but honestly, it took me a long time to understand that.

In Brussels we had bought a nice apartment in a central part of the city and when we were looking, the agencies followed up for us and the banks offered us a mortgage without any problem. I was a lawyer with a good job and my husband an engineer with a great permanent work contract. We were young, and we were considered a safe bet.

In Geneva, the bank had looked down on us, saying we were nuts to hope to buy a villa with such a low budget. And my husband's salary, which to us seemed to be enormous, was not enough to offer any guarantee. The house prices were crazy. Mistreated from the first time we entered a Swiss bank, we were praying to find someone willing to offer us a mortgage. Our business with them simply wasn't interesting; our buying power was drastically and irredeemably diminished. I realised again that I was not, in fact, on vacation but that the increase in my husband's salary was fundamental, not to increase our standard of living in respect to Brussels, but simply to survive on Swiss territory.

We Buy a House

Bellicose, impatient and neurotic (never a winning combination) and with some help from my architect father, we finally managed to buy a small terraced house, about ten kilometres from the centre of Geneva. The house was situated in a village by the lake, with the train station practically in our garden. It was one of those cases where in Bari we would think that people living there had enormous financial problems, perhaps the father was an alcoholic and the mother had a hard life. We had invested all our savings and we had managed to buy this little yellow and green terraced house.

In fact, when we made our tax return, it turned out that families with economic disadvantages were indeed expected to live there with the noise of the trains passing the garden every seven minutes, shaking the windows of the house. For that reason, we had to pay very low taxes on the property. It was the least the state could do: compensate us for having the courage to spend a crazy amount of money on a house like that. Every time a train passed, the lights in the living room went off.

The presence of an atomic bunker in our home, even though it was such a tiny house, really surprised me. The atomic bunker is a completely Helvetic peculiarity. According to federal law, all the inhabitants must have access to an atomic bunker in case of world war, or of the explosion of one of the nuclear power stations in the area.

In our new house, the bunker was next to the storage room in the cellar. It is also obligatory, in the case of an atomic emergency or if nuclear war is declared, to play host to your neighbours who might lack such a shelter. This obligation was even written into our contract to buy the house. Our neighbours were not particularly nice... so, imagining the scenario of a nuclear war or a nuclear explosion, I could choose to save the lives of my family, fleeing terrified from Bari and Amsterdam, or those of my dear neighbours.

In those circumstances, I couldn't see any way in which the Swiss authorities could exercise any control. Who could possibly come and check whether I had given shelter to my neighbours?

Our bunker immediately found a less catastrophic function: it became the ideal storage room for wine, sauces, preserves and sausages from Italy.

In any case, it's reassuring to know that in case of a nuclear world war, the only ones to survive the deadly radiation would be the inhabitants of the Helvetic Confederation.

The Fines

Budgeting for Fines

In a short time we realised that the cost of living in Switzerland was really high. One of the accounting entries that negatively influenced our family budget was, undoubtedly, fines. Probably because of my indisciplined Barese behaviour, or Harold's improvised parking, we were persecuted by fines. They were always pecking at us, and I mean always! And they were certainly well organised. It seemed as though the traffic police were following us day and night realising that we were an easy target. We were already aware of the efficiency of the police, but this seemed exaggerated to us.

My muse is called Felix: my dearest friend from Malaga. It was he who had introduced me to my husband in Brussels ten years before. Felix, after a long period of living in Brussels, had been transferred to Geneva a year before us. I remembered that shortly before our move, Felix explained to us:
'In your first year in Switzerland you should plan for a budget of at least 1,500 Swiss Francs for the fines. In your second year it will get better, you will know how things work and then you'll pay more attention.'
My husband laughed and replied:
'Go on, maybe because you come from the south of Spain! But you have to realise that I am Dutch and so I'm used to driving very carefully. In Holland the traffic police are very serious, and I know exactly how to behave.'
In our first year living in Geneva we had to pay 2,000 Swiss Francs just in fines. Felix's calculation had been optimistic!

I think we live in the country with the highest number of fines per head. On the other hand, perhaps the Swiss orderliness that borders on perfection must exact some sacrifices on the part of the community. Just imagine in Bari I used to double-park outside a shop while I chatted with the shopkeeper. The police would arrive and the shopkeeper would tell the police that I was in his shop, and I wouldn't get a fine. Two different planets.

The civic sense of the citizens of the Helvetic territory is very distinct. This characteristic has its good sides but sometimes it has some very bad ones. For those who come from a country in which the civic sense is not so strong it's not easy to adjust... You need a settling-in period. A very expensive settling-in period.

Informing, or Spy versus Spy

But are the police really everywhere? How else could they be hassling us all the time?

The national sport, practised constantly and assiduously by a considerable part of the population, is informing. Informing is a very Swiss peculiarity.

Let me explain this better. This is a country overpopulated with spies, always alert, trying to observe other people's affairs and proud to denounce others to the authorities each and every time an inhabitant strays in respect to the laws of the land, even the most insignificant and silly. The spies are the watchdogs of the legal system and are present everywhere, in places and at times you can't believe. They hide themselves and then pop up and suddenly you find yourself in confrontation with the relevant authorities. You feel persecuted, always under the control of neighbours, colleagues and passers-by who are never minding their own business.

Since I was very small I was taught that someone who spies on others is vile and should be nicknamed Judas for the rest of his life. For a woman from the South of Italy, the country of *omertà* in which no one has ever heard or seen anything, to live in such a mirror-image reality, excessively populated with curious spies, isn't easy. The training to become a good spy begins at a tender age: five-years-old. In fact, during the first years at school, the good Helvetic schoolteachers teach the children to denounce their classmates, a training reinforced by the school body. Informing on others was the most evident characteristic of my host country and in my opinion the most difficult to accept. It was certainly the one which provoked the most primitive instincts, the most secret desires: to catch the informer red-handed and beat him to a pulp.

To recognise, digest and accept this bizarre habit, took me a long, long time. The truth is that there are a large number of trained informants in and around Geneva.

I had already heard about the 'civil spy service' before moving here while I was still unsuspecting. I had contacted Francesca, a girl from Milan, mother of three children, who had lived for several years in Geneva, to ask for information regarding looking for a babysitter. I didn't know Francesca directly; she was the daughter of a friend of my mother's. But based on previous experience of my mother's friends, this was no guarantee of her reliability.

During our telephone conversation, Francesca told me: 'Finding a babysitter is not difficult but many are illegal immigrants. Normally it's difficult to find people with the right documents and they are very expensive. You are risking a big fine if you employ an illegal immigrant. My babysitter is illegal and I never let her go out into the garden of our villa or our neighbours would see her and she might be denounced. Remember; deny everything to your neighbours. Never let them know you have an illegal immigrant in your house.'

(Now, I like to reflect that the neighbours Francesca was talking about are the same ones that you have to put up with in the bunker in the case of an unexpected nuclear explosion.)

I thanked her and ended the conversation rapidly. A bit shocked and alarmed at her story, I thought that Francesca must have been the victim of a persecution complex.

After the phone call my husband said to me:

'Was Francesca nice, will you call her when we get there?'

'No, she seemed to me to be half mad. She was talking about spies who live next to her house. She must be one of those people who feel like they are always being persecuted, a woman with lots of problems and strange phobias.'

Once I arrived I never called her back. I try not to frequent psychopaths.

Only two years after moving to Geneva, I also talked just like Francesca to the new arrivals.

The Bank

During the first months that we lived in Geneva, we were in and out of the bank trying to arrange our mortgage. One morning we were going to the bank simply to get a form, so the visit was going to be brief. All the parking spaces next to the building were taken, while the neighbouring parking lot for the clients of PricewaterHouseCoopers was almost empty, about twenty spaces. The same building housed both the bank and PricewaterHouseCoopers.

Knowing that the visit would be brief, I parked the car in one of the PricewaterHouseCoopers spaces. We hurried towards the bank, got the form and within a couple of minutes we returned. On the windscreen was a ticket. We looked at it incredulously:

'We have been advised that you have been visiting the offices of the bank. You are not allowed to park in the spaces reserved for clients of PricewaterHouseCoopers. Please pay us 80 Swiss Francs.'

We looked around with suspicion; without doubt the spy was still lying in wait. We observed the passers-by to try and meet the gaze of the spy. The informer had had the time to check the reason for our visit and to call the traffic police. All in two minutes. Another basic characteristic of the local spies is that they act with impressive speed, also to avoid contact with the 'injured party'. And, even more incredible, they manage to find a traffic warden nearby who is ready to strike like lightning. The cowardly informer had made his get-away, or disappeared, content to have done the duty of a good citizen.

The Cash Machine

I was in the car with Alice looking for a cash machine and a parking place. We had just bought a Renault Espace, one of those enormous cars ideal for a big family. Now, I would be the first to admit that I can't drive like Michael Schumacher, and with a car of those dimensions, I naturally had some difficulties parking it.

Alice was sitting in her car seat and crying desperately. I, after having made about eighty-five manoeuvres to park and having risked spraining my wrist and elbow, parked the car and got out covered in sweat. I released the straps of the car seat and finally picked Alice up and held her to stop her crying.

Suddenly I heard a lady shouting at me indignantly that I had parked my car badly. I must have looked nonplussed. Then I saw the woman pointing to the ground with her hand and I looked closer. My back right wheel was misplaced by two centimetres; I mean two centimetres over the white line that marked out the parking place.

Irritated and tired by the parking manoeuvres, I said to her:

'Madame, I'm only going to be here for a couple of minutes. I need to get money from the cash machine. I don't understand why you're so upset. I'm not in anyone's way and the other cars can get by without a problem.'

This concrete and practical reply would be typical from someone raised in the chaotic streets of Bari. I couldn't imagine getting upset about the two centimetres my tyre was beyond the white line. Honesty, if that kind lady hadn't drawn my attention to it, I would never have noticed.

I was away for only five minutes. When I came back I found a traffic warden placing a ticket under my windscreen wiper.

Agitated, I ran to the traffic warden and set about him, saying:

'Please don't give me a fine I've only been here five minutes, it's absurd.'

I was aware that my request was useless. Flexibility cannot exist in a country where everything is rigorously in the right place. The walls by the side of the street are clean, not graffitied; the flowers are perfectly arranged and the green lawns have grass cut to just the right length.

'I have received a denunciation from the lady that was parked behind you. She had come to look for me in the police station opposite. When we receive a denunciation from a third party we are obliged to levy a fine.'

Horrified, I searched for the lady, screwing up my eyes in concentration.

My curiosity was aroused. Where was that lady, doubtless a practitioner of the oldest profession in the world? No, that was unfair. Where was the lady — daughter of peasants — who was clearly an expert practitioner of the oldest profession in the world? But the informant had vaporised into thin air and I returned home depressed.

I became, after the first few months of conflict, very disciplined. I knew that if I parked my car, at any time of day or night, in a forest, or in the most abandoned spot in Geneva, there was always a potential danger: a traffic warden could appear from nowhere and give me a fine. I became a woman with a strong civic sense.

Informants work.

Watch out... for Helping Others

The story that I am going to tell you is absolutely the most incredible and incomprehensible that I have ever heard. This is not an urban legend that foreigners tell about Geneva. It is completely true. My friend Loreto from Granada lived in an apartment block in the centre with her husband David and their three children. David was a colleague of my husband's and a workaholic.

One night at about four in the morning someone knocked on the door of their apartment. David, quite alarmed, opened the door. It was his Swiss neighbour, a man of about eighty who, with a worried voice, told him:

'My wife isn't feeling well, and I am too worked up to drive the car and take her to hospital. Please, could you drive us to the hospital?'

'Stay calm and don't worry, I'll get dressed and take you immediately.'

David got dressed quickly, explained to his wife that he was taking the neighbours to the hospital, and hurried out. Because of the urgency, David decided to drive the wrong way down a 20 metre section of road, to go around a one-way zone that would have made the journey longer. In a few minutes they arrived at the hospital and the old couple got out of David's car. They thanked him. And David, exhausted, went back home to bed.

A week later Loreto and David received a huge fine from the police for driving the wrong way down a one-way road on the night of the incident. David was dumbfounded and reassured Loreto that no police patrol had seen them that night. The streets were deserted at four in the morning; they hadn't seen a soul during their trip to the hospital.

Several days later David met the old lady on the landing of the apartment block. She was no longer ill and had been discharged from the hospital. David told her that he had received a big fine.

The ex-patient scolded:

'My husband had to alert the police. You do realise that we're not living in Spain and that the rules must be respected? We clearly saw that you drove the wrong way down rue Mozart. Don't you know that that's illegal?'

The Neighbours

A Housewarming Gift

It was cold and snowing on the day we moved into our new home. Finally, we could move into our small yellow and green house with the trains at the end of the garden. I tried not to over-dramatise the negative aspects and told myself it was perfect: I could always take a train and I would be in the city centre in the blink of an eye.

We were happy to change house, because now we had a garden for our children and we had all our furniture which had been in storage for several months. Living without your own belongings for several months is like never being in your own home.

Together with all the packing cases was my blue Nissan Micra, bought in Brussels seven years earlier and which had remained in Belgium until our move was finalised.

I moved house on the same day that my father moved to a new villa near to Bari. At the end of the day he called to tell me how it had gone.

My father said:

'We are really tired, but luckily we don't need to cook dinner tonight. Our new neighbours gave us home-made focaccia as a welcome gesture.'

I compared:

'We're also exhausted and our neighbours also came to see us. They wanted us to know that we shouldn't leave the rubbish bin in front of the house. It seems that there is a collection bin for all the residents' rubbish a hundred metres away.'

After all, we were not in Bari where you could leave your rubbish bin in front of your apartment for days on end and no one would protest. The great Swiss civic sense again. It was me who had decided to live in the well-organised north, so I couldn't well complain that our welcome from the neighbours was a rebuke for my negligence.

The next day we woke up to a house full of boxes which had to be emptied. I was alone with the children, since our Paraguayan babysitter, Fanny, had been acting strangely for several weeks. Fanny was very preoccupied – she had fallen in love. She had fallen for a two metre tall Nigerian boy with a big sports car. I don't know why but it didn't inspire me with a lot of confidence....

A couple with a Rottweiler dog had lived for several years in the house before us. We found lots of that wonderful dog's excrement in the garden. The people who had sold us the house hadn't even bothered to clean up the garden, probably they hadn't even noticed. In fact, on the day of our move, the grass was completely covered in snow, and it was only when this had thawed they we recognised what we had inherited from the dog.

Our neighbours were of Spanish origin, but second generation Swiss. They were not noted in the area for their class or refinement but very friendly. They loved to barbecue and whenever the weather permitted Carlos would come out, bare-chested, and light up the charcoal. There was no fence between our garden and his, so we were obliged to admire Carlos' love handles, since he weighed about 150 kilos. We often saw his wife in the garden in her pyjamas, watering the plants every day. All in all, we were living in a silent community – often in the very same garden all together, but without addressing a word to one another.

In the other houses lived young families like us – people who had moved recently to Geneva and who came from various countries. In house number 6 lived a lovely couple: she was Thai and he Spanish with a beautiful bilingual daughter. We nicknamed him the Basque terrorist from ETA because of his shifty looks. In fact he was a gentle soul, who would not have hurt a fly. Both of them worked for international organisations and had lived in other countries before settling in Switzerland. With them we struck up an immediate friendship, which was a blessing.

Obscene Acts in Public Places

After a week of living in our new house, my neighbour Lidia, a second-generation Swiss of Italian origins, knocked on my door.

With a suspicious expression, she whispered in French:

'Excuse me if I'm disturbing you but we met two days ago. I'm your neighbour from house number 1, the nearest to the railway station. We need to speak; could you come to my house as soon as possible?'

Yes, I had seen her before. I had asked myself how anyone could live so close to the railway lines. If a passenger absent-mindedly threw a carton out of the train window it would have landed right in her garden. And if the train driver were distracted and made a mistake coming into the station, he would have ended up in her living room.

'Certainly, do you want to come in? Would you like some tea?'

Hospitality is sacred in South-Italy, and I try to keep up the tradition.

'No thank you, I would prefer it if you came to my house, I really need to speak to you urgently.'

I left my children with Fanny and followed her to her house. The living room was spotless and orderly; a strong smell of cleaning products hung in the room. I settled myself comfortably in one of her brown sofas. The room was practically empty. No pictures, no ornaments. I didn't feel at ease. But I was happy; I thought that Lidia might become a new friend.

Lidia questioned:

'The girl that comes to you every day, does she help with the cleaning?'

'Yes, you know I have two small children and the house has four floors, so I need a bit of help...'

I was trying to use a slightly confidential tone, thinking I was speaking with another mother who would understand me. She retorted quickly:

'I have three children and I have never needed any help, I've always done everything myself... anyway... I need to tell you that the girl

52

who works in your house has been committing obscene acts in front of the windows of my house. My children and I saw her and her lover kissing passionately in his car from the living room window. My children could see everything! I would like you to talk with her or the next time it happens I will call the police. Are they legal? I'm sure that he, the coloured boy, is an illegal immigrant. Am I right? If I call the police, they will check their residence permits and if they are illegal they will both be thrown out of the country immediately.'

Fortunately Fanny had her papers in order, since she had a Spanish passport. As for her boyfriend, I had no idea. I started to get worried; I felt a cold sweat as the advice of Francesca, the daughter of my mother's friend, returned to my mind. 'Deny everything; deny everything to your neighbours.' (And I had not trusted Francesca…)

I should not have needed to worry; our babysitter was legal, but maybe not her boyfriend. But I didn't want Fanny to be unhappy on account of my nosy neighbour. Then I said to myself: no, Lidia was Italian, only second generation Swiss, and we Italians couldn't imagine doing something like that, denouncing somebody… no it was unimaginable. I tried to seem friendly, nice and scandalised at her story and said to her:

'I can't believe that they were kissing in her boyfriend's car in front of your house. That's terrible; I will talk to her immediately and make sure it doesn't happen again. But how old are your children?'

'My son is 16 and my daughter 20.'

I thanked her and went away incredulous and agitated. Once I was back home I talked with Fanny and she assured me that in future she would be more discreet when snogging with her Nigerian boyfriend. I suddenly felt spied upon by my neighbour, an Italian housewife. Was it possible that her children, in the flower of youth, had nothing better to do than peek at Fanny through the living room window? What an odd family and Lidia, my compatriot, was wretched. She hadn't even asked me where I came from in Italy. And why had she continued talking to me in French?

Mowing the Lawn

This was the first time we had found ourselves with a small garden to look after – it required a minimum of effort to keep in order. I, alone with the children all week, had neither the time nor the inclination to take it on. Amongst other things, Fanny had disappeared with her boyfriend for a week without telling me and so we had been forced to fire her.

I hoped my husband Harold, considering his Dutch origins, would have green fingers – he had always lived in houses with big gardens. But I was wrong. Like me, he had no idea where to begin. After several hours trailing around several garden centres, we managed to buy a lawnmower, the cheapest possible. We spent nearly all that Saturday in various garden shops.

Harold, enthusiastic at his new acquisition, started to cut the grass early on Sunday morning. Stressed and sweating, he was having difficulty to get the complicated machine to work properly. After several attempts, the lawnmower started to do the job it was designed for. Harold was satisfied and happy to have succeeded. Soon after, in the middle of this laborious work, someone knocked on the door. I peeped out of the kitchen window and saw it was a policeman. What was a policeman doing at our house?

We hadn't ever done anything wrong. Through my mind went one of those film scenes where the wife opens the door to suddenly discover after years of marriage that her husband was a con-man, or worse, an assassin. Or perhaps Harold was involved in trafficking narcotics or was associated with gangsters. I was really worried.

I tried to calm myself and reasoned that if my husband really did have a second life as a gangster, we would have been a lot richer than we were, and we wouldn't be living in a tiny house with trains at the end of the garden. I quickly imagined those films in which the surprised wife opens the door of an immense and splendid villa – but that was not our case, so Harold was innocent.

I looked out into the garden and gestured to him to turn off the noisy machine and told him that the police were at the door. Harold didn't seem very worried, just astonished. I reckoned if he had done anything serious he would be looking a lot more perplexed. To be honest, he goes as red as a tomato whenever he tells any kind of lie and since he is practically albino, his face really changes colour. If he had been lying to me for the last ten years I think I would have caught on. He didn't have the guilty look of a criminal…

Bathed in sweat, Harold looked at me and turned off the lawnmower. He looked me in the eyes and then, with a strong Barese accent, and gesticulating like an Italian, asked me:

'What on earth do they want?'

Poor, innocent Harold, if he only knew the things I had been thinking about him…

Together we opened the door for the policeman.

The policeman informed us of the reason for his visit:

'One of your neighbours has contacted us to let us know that you have been cutting the grass on a Sunday.'

Harold and I did not understand so I quickly said:

'I'm sorry but I can't quite understand why our neighbour has contacted you? What's the problem with cutting the grass on a Sunday?'

'According to local law, it is forbidden to cut the grass on a Sunday and you are risking a fine.'

But our neighbour could have come to us to say this instead of contacting the police. And so now the police were at my house because we were cutting the grass on a Sunday? No. Not possible – I must have misunderstood.

'Excuse me; you came here to our house just to tell us that?'

'Madame, are you aware that you have violated the bylaws of the commune? After all, we are not in Italy where everything is a mess. Here we obey the rules, and if not, the police intervene.'

How did he know I was Italian? Had the spying neighbour also said that? We Italians often criticise and speak badly of our country but we can't stand it when a foreigner does it. I immediately took a dislike to the policeman, but I had learned by painful experience that sometimes it is better to suppress such feelings, to avoid more trouble later on.

Even if his reasoning was flawless, it left us horrified. Can you imagine if the police intervened in Bari every time someone violated a rule or a bylaw? The combined armed forces of the entire European Union would not be enough. In that instant, I could not have looked myself in the mirror, but I was sure I had my classic gormless expression with a half-open mouth.

I tried to hide my amazement and contempt, and, with an exaggerated and false politeness I apologised to the policeman, hoping to avoid a heavy fine:

'I'm mortified! We've just arrived here and we don't know all of the rules. I can assure you that we were not familiar with this prohibition or we would never have allowed ourselves to disturb our neighbours.'

'This time I will not give you a fine. But it is the duty of each responsible citizen to inform himself about the applicable laws in the country in which he lives. Please read the local bylaws with attention.'

As soon as the policeman had gone, I made a brief internet search. In fact, according to the law it is forbidden to cut the grass on a Sunday to prevent a breach of the peace and to preserve public order. I also found a paragraph in the same law which said:

'Actions that could disturb public order and peace are forbidden, in particular: riot, making excessive noise, bawdy singing whether inside a private dwelling or nearby.'

The rule not only referred to Sundays and holidays but to every day of the year.

So if I wanted to sing "Frère Jacques" at the top of my voice with my children in my own house, the police could intervene and maybe hand everyone a fine? I couldn't breathe for a moment. But then it surely couldn't be that all the laws were applied to the letter?

Which of the neighbours had called the police? If they had talked to us, we would have stopped cutting the grass. But by then, given the tiny dimensions of our garden, we would already have finished.

The months passed and our life went on happily in our little house. Harold had rapidly lost interest in gardening and in our lawn. So in a short space of time, our garden took on a neglected aspect, like a little jungle. Our next-door neighbours, Carlos and Mariangeles, kept their garden perfectly. She, in her pyjamas, spent hours watering his roses. I suppressed my feelings of guilt, remembering that their children were already adolescents, whereas I had two small children to look after, which left me little time for roses.

Next to the front door of our house was a tiny area of grass of about 8 square metres, shared with Mariangeles and Carlos. There was no fence or division, so we took turns cutting the grass. During the summer I was in Puglia for two months and Harold had to make a lot of business trips. Returning from vacation I found the 8 square meters of grass in a bizarre state. On our side, the grass was tall and shaggy, whilst on the side of the second generation Spanish-Swiss it was perfectly cut. Taking into account the dimensions of the small lawn it must have been quite difficult to leave half of it uncut. Without doubt, it had been harder to cut half the grass than to cut all of it. I could not understand their reason for doing this. Perplexed, I knocked on their door to ask for the explanation. Mariangeles reprimanded me:

'We are tired of always having to cut your side of the lawn. From now on each of us will cut his own side.'

'You are right, I'm sorry, but I was away with my children in Italy and Harold was on business trips and then he spent his vacation with us. Don't worry; we will make this up to you. If you like, we can cut all of the grass for the next two months to recuperate the time you have lost.'

Cold and dry, she responded:

'Absolutely not. Each one will cut his own side, I don't believe it will work any other way, you two are not methodical enough.'

To be honest, I could not truthfully contradict her, but I wanted to recover the situation and I said:

'I promise you that we will pay attention. After all, our lawnmower is quite large for this small patch of ground. In the end it will be easier to cut the whole area that just half.'

She replied:

'I realise that this will be difficult for us as well, but my husband and I have made a decision. Each one will cut his own side of the grass and the matter is closed.'

She said goodbye coldly and closed the door in my face. I felt bad, really bad. I had always had a good relationship with Mariangeles which was now ruined thanks to a small patch of uncut lawn... From that moment my relations with her were still courteous, but much colder. During the three years that we stayed in that house we continued to cut all of the grass in front. They, in contrast, always cut exactly half of it.

Parking

Our Italian-Swiss neighbours, Lidia and Francesco Giotti, had two parking places, but they only used one because she didn't drive and they only had one car. In the whole of the housing estate, there were only five spaces designated for guests.

One evening I organised a party at our house and invited several Argentinean and Uruguayan friends. One of their husbands parked his car, on my instructions, in one of Francesco's spaces, which seemed a good idea to me, since this parking place was always unoccupied. The Giotti family, for whatever reason, did not often have visitors, and I was sure that their second space would not be needed. On the other hand, we often had a house full of people. All the parking spaces for guests were already occupied.

At a certain point in the evening, Francesco Giotti knocked on our door. Harold opened and Francesco yelled at him:

'Somebody has parked in one of my spaces; he must move his car immediately.'

'But sorry M. Giotti, you only have one car and the other space is always empty. We are celebrating my wife's birthday today and we have a lot of guests in the house. We didn't know where they could all park, and that's why we thought we could take advantage of your spare space.'

'Well, you thought wrong, very wrong. The parking space is mine and it must remain free at all times. If the person who parked their car in my place doesn't move it within a minute, I will call the police.'

The neighbour left in a fury, leaving Harold in a state of shock. Fabio, our Argentinean friend, looked at us disconcertedly and moved his car rapidly.

From that day on, Mr Giotti parked his one car sideways on his two spaces, blocking both of them.

The police would come because we had parked on the space of a neighbour? It really is a fixation to call the long-suffering policemen. The poor things must never have a moment's peace. They must come home from work and their wife asks them:

'Everything OK at work today, Honey?'

'Yes dear, I was a hero. I had to intervene because a neighbour had occupied the parking spot of another neighbour. And then I had to stop an Italian cutting the grass on Sunday.'

The Letter from the Commune

After a year of living in our new house, we received a polite letter from the commune in which we were living, signed by the mayor.

The contents of the letter were as follows:

'For several months we have received many complaints about you on the part of the residents of your housing estate. The complaints concern making excessive noise in the neighbourhood, using the lawnmower outside of the times allowed by the law, neglect of the lawns and for the registration of your cars. Your cars are currently registered to the Canton of Geneva whereas they must be registered to your address in the Canton of Vaud. Controls will be taking place in the next few days and we hope that we will not have to report anyone. The communal police are at your disposal from 07.00 until 20.00 to collaborate on maintaining public order and to prevent disturbances of the neighbours. Yours sincerely.'

Let's see who all the guilty parties were:
- cutting the grass on Sunday (us and our Thai neighbour);
- car not registered to the Canton of Vaud (Tunisian and Spanish neighbours);
- excessive noise (us and our Tunisian neighbour).

So the whole community of foreign residents in the housing estate had been caught in one go. No one had been spared, they had got us all.

In the list of miscreants there were no Swiss; their civic sense is admirable!

Eight Months Earlier in Brussels...

In Brussels we lived in a newly-built apartment block in which the average age was about 75. Young couples with children would normally live in a detached house, but having lots of nice grannies around for my children wasn't so bad. All of them asked how I was getting on with my pregnancy, they offered to hold Dante for me and they were always ready to chat with me just to pass the time. The lady who lived on the first floor, Jeanine, a lovely Belgian pensioner, told me every time she saw me towards the end of my pregnancy with Alice, that when she was young she had had six children, three boys and three girls.

While giving birth to each of the three girls, she had had problems which resulted in none of them surviving. But the three boys, on the other hand, had enjoyed perfect health. She kept on recounting this story and then telling me:
'We hope that things go better with you, and that you don't lose your daughters like I did.' Great... even leaving aside the fact that I am an anxious, superstitious hypochondriac and I was haunted by the memory of my previous birth. Even worse, my friendly Brussels gynaecologist looked like a crazy artist with his long, thick blonde hair.

The problem was that Jeanine, every time she saw me, forgot that she had told me the story of her births the day before and started with the whole thing again. But I could have rationalised the problem: Jeanine had given birth 40 years before and medical science had made gigantic strides in the meantime, so this should not have been a reason for me to get so worried.

In our apartment block there also lived a divorced Danish alcoholic who often fell down the stairs. One evening I was alone at home and I found him in front of my door bleeding and babbling in Danish. One shout was enough and my adorable fellow-tenants came to my aid and took him to hospital. Such a great solidarity and humanity was the rule in that block. It had seemed to me normal and not a luxury.

Punctuality

The Importance of Punctuality

We had been living in Geneva for a year and finally we had made some new friends. When we are abroad we Italians always seek each other out, and in fact I had now tracked down other Italian women who had chosen to live here as desperate housewives like me. I don't know why, but Dutchmen, on the other hand, hardly ever go looking for each other.

By now I could find my way around by car, and I was getting used to the habits and customs of the locals. I quickly realised that if you want to live happily in this country, you need to be punctual. Let me be clear about this: you *always* need to arrive on time.
From when I was a small child, punctuality was an alien concept to me. My mother is one of those people who always arrives late. When I was a little girl I don't think I ever arrived at school, dance or piano lessons on time, and nobody ever batted an eyelid. When friends would come to pick up my mother and she would always reply:
'I'm ready. I'll be right down.'
Actually, she was still deciding what to wear.
For me, punctuality is an abstract concept. I suffer from a chronic tendency to be late. I even arrived late at my own graduation. The chairman of the Degree Commission had already called out my name and I wasn't in the room; I was out in the corridor chatting with friends. I still got a good mark, though.
I have a dear friend, Sergio. Whenever my friends and I arrived outside his apartment block and rang his bell, he would declare:
'I'm on my way down… be with you in a minute.'
He would then return to the TV programme he was watching and only come down when it had finished. We undoubtedly complained at times, but for us it didn't change the fact he was a dear friend.
For the Swiss, being punctual is as important as eating well is for the Italians. Tardiness is simply not tolerated. If you are so much as five minutes late, the gynaecologist will cancel your appointment, no

matter how virulent your infection, and the dentist will have no qualms about leaving you to endure the agony of a raging toothache. This was a problem for me right from the start. It is worth pointing out that my husband, after an initial phase of irritation and incredulity, has learned to put up with my lateness, and even my Dutch in-laws – after years of suffering – have wised-up and learned how to deal with it. They'll book a restaurant for half past six (Dutch dinner time) and tell me that the reservation is for six p.m. I have caught on now, of course, but I don't say anything and that way everyone is happy. In Brussels people are fairly indulgent towards latecomers, but in Switzerland it is a totally different story. After a year of education and training in Swiss punctuality, after seeing my husband suffer attacks of hysteria and risk cardiac arrest, after countless birthday parties missed, I am a changed woman: I now arrive on time! This is not simply incredible – it is a real miracle.

The Fancy Dress Party

My first punctuality faux-pas occurred when my Swiss neighbour, Celine, invited us to a fancy dress party for her daughter's birthday. The party began at two in the afternoon and as Alice was still sleeping I didn't want to wake her. I should point out that at this stage my children didn't have many friends yet and the event was a chance to remedy this. They were happy and excited at the prospect of going to a party. However, convinced that the celebrations would go on till about seven and that we had plenty of time to get there, I let Alice sleep on, and it was 4 p.m. when we eventually knocked at the door. Celine opened up, astonished to see us. Alice was dressed as a princess and Dante was a pirate clutching a present.

'Why so late?' she asked me.

'The party is over and all the other children have gone home. Didn't you read the invitation? It was written on it: two till three thirty.'

I must have had one of my typical gormless looks on my face at this point. Somehow I managed to blurt out:

'I'm sorry. It's just that Alice was sleeping and I hadn't read the hours on the invitation properly. We're really sorry. At least let us give you Caroline's present.'

It was extremely embarrassing and five minutes later we left. Alice and Dante were crying and inconsolably sad, and as we headed home I felt depressed and disillusioned. I also felt guilty, and this wasn't helped when we got home by my husband scolding:

'You're not in Bari now, you know. You have to respect the times people tell you. Look, it clearly says on the invitation that the party was due to finish at half past three. It's the same in Holland. People write the start *and* the end time for a party. If you want to live in northern Europe, you have to take that on board! And of *course* the kids are going to cry if you mess up and they miss the fancy dress party they've been looking forward to. As usual, it's down to your chronic lateness.'

'It seems ridiculous to me to organise a party for just an hour and a half, and I'm sorry but it doesn't seem like very good manners to put in writing what time people should leave your house. It's like you want to kick them out. It's downright rude. When we organise parties we would never dream of doing such a thing.'

'WE... WE... WE... Nonsense! If you don't accept that this is the way things are here, you're always going to have problems. Try and get it into your head. Brussels was different, I know, but we're living in Geneva now and you have to adapt.'

Unfortunately, he was right. For our wedding we had organised a big party in Holland at Harold's parents' place. Thinking back, I remembered now that the invitation said the party would start at three and finish at six. At 3 p.m. people were queuing at the door to get in, and by six they had all left.

For Harold, Geneva was less of a culture shock than it was for me. For a Southern Italian it would be inconceivable to put a leaving time on an invitation; people would think you were joking.

The Neapolitan Shopkeeper

In the little village where we live there is a chemist, a mini-market and a video shop: a rather depressing scenario for a person used to living in a city. Anyway, one evening I decided to rent a film and headed for the video store. The shop was well-stocked and I was delighted to see that there was a selection of Italian films. I started talking to the owner and it turned out he was of Neapolitan origins, so we started speaking Italian. His Italian was dreadful (that French "r"!) but he was clearly happy to get an opportunity to speak it. He appeared to be very proud of his connection with Naples, and he waxed lyrical about his love of southern Italy. I chose a film, paid for it and returned home thinking about what a small world it was: fancy finding a Neapolitan in this little Swiss village. The next day at five past seven I took the film back to the video shop, where my new Neapolitan friend curtly reprimanded me in French:

'You were supposed to bring the film back by seven this evening. As you can see on the sign behind me, films have to be returned by 7 p.m. the following day. As it is now five past seven, you're going to have to pay me for the extra day.'

'You're joking, of course! We're talking about five minutes... But this is ridiculous... How can you be so inflexible? Listen, do me a favour and never talk about being a Neapolitan again. In the south of Italy we're famous for our flexibility. There's not an ounce of southern Italian left in you. I'm not going to pay you the extra money. Call the police if you want. I will never set foot in your shop again.'

Renting a film in Switzerland is already expensive enough without paying double for being five minutes late.

I was extremely worked up and the shopkeeper – evidently in a state of shock – was dumbstruck. I stormed out, banging the door behind me. I don't really know what got into me. But how could a

Neapolitan, of all people, get infected by that intolerance, and pettiness? He had truly been cut off from his ancient roots. On other occasions too, I have noticed that the Italian, Spanish and Greek immigrants who have grown up here are more Swiss than the Swiss, and they are the ones whose inflexibility will leave you open-mouthed in astonishment.

The Christmas Concert

If I had any doubts about the need to be punctual, then Dante's Christmas concert convinced me once and for all that there was nothing for it but to start arriving on time. Dante was two and a half and attending a local nursery. The concert was due to start at 9 a.m., and, after carefully dressing the children, I began to get myself ready while my husband sorted out the cameras. Dante was going through a phase of acute shyness but Harold was really looking forward to seeing his son sing in French. Determined to look my best for the occasion, I took great pains with my make-up and put on a particularly beautiful dress. Harold, unable to stop looking at his watch, started grumbling:

'Come on, get a move on, we're going to be late. You know how difficult it is to park near the school. I don't want to be late.'

Slipping on my earrings, I replied:

'Harold, you're getting worked up about nothing as usual. We'll find a parking space, don't worry. I'll be ready in a minute. And apart from anything else, do you have any idea how long it takes to organise three classes of children for a Christmas concert? They'll never start on time.'

We got to the school at ten past nine, and Harold, sweating and angry, dropped us off and went to look for somewhere to park. My husband always gets anxious and muddled when he has to find a parking space. Usually when we go out, his first question – and you can hear the worry in his voice – is:

'Yes, okay, we'll go, but where am I going to park?'

His father has the same phobia, and to be honest, I've never understood why they get so het up about parking…

I should mention at this point that Harold had taken a half day off to see Dante's show.

Holding the children's hands, I ran into the main hall. All of Dante's classmates were wearing Father Christmas hats and singing. As soon as we entered, all the parents turned round and looked at me contemptuously. You could see what they were thinking: how could you arrive late for the children's concert? I walked past the children and parents and pushed my son towards the teacher, who stood him on a chair. Dante was red as a beetroot with shame.

Heaving a sigh of relief, I was settling back to enjoy the show when it suddenly struck me that something was wrong. All the children were dressed from head to toe in red. Dante, on the other hand, was sporting a smart blue suit. The poor child was so mortified he couldn't even open his mouth to sing and it was only with the greatest difficulty that he was holding back the tears. I took the invitation out of my bag and read it through. It did indeed say that the children should wear red that morning, and I hadn't realised. I looked around for my husband. He finally made it into the room for the last verse of the last song.

At the buffet after the show, Harold realised that Dante was the only child dressed in blue. Fortunately, he is a husband with a great sense of humour, and he saved me further embarrassment by seeing the funny side of it. A few minutes later, though, rage got the better of him and he suddenly walked out. For two days he wouldn't speak to me and I was consumed with guilt for having embarrassed my son and angered my husband. In effect, when they write on an invitation in Switzerland that the Christmas party is to begin at nine, it begins at nine. Ever since then, every time my children have been involved in some kind of show, I have been there ten minutes early. It's hard to believe but I really have become punctual!

The School

A Bilingual Family

We are one of countless bilingual families living in Geneva. When I was pregnant with Dante, one of the ways I tried to calm my anxieties was by reading about the best way to bring up bilingual children. Illustrious professors from the University of Oxford advise that each parent should always use only his or her mother-tongue when speaking to the children. We have followed this advice to the letter and, in fact, both our children are bilingual and quite content to be so.

Harold and I, on the other hand, have both experienced problems on account of our patriotic instincts. There has always been a certain element of competition between us, along the lines of:

'Dante which language do you prefer: Italian or Dutch?' or

'Do you prefer Holland or Italy?'

And we look at him nervously, staring into his eyes in the hope of convincing him to give the right answer. Children, of course, are often more intelligent than their parents. Dante has always teasingly answered:

'Both'.

One of my biggest disappointments came when Dante spoke his first word. He was only one at the time, and was playing with a toy cow in the living room while Harold and I were watching television. Suddenly Dante said:

'Cu.'

I didn't react, but Harold leapt onto the sofa and shouted:

'Dante has started talking, did you hear? He said his first word! Can you believe it? Dante can talk! He can talk! He said "Cu!"'

'Harold, what have you been drinking? The child only said "cu"; it's no different from when he says "la" or "ba". That's not talking. At his age children communicate in monosyllables. They're not proper words.'

'You don't understand. He said it while he was holding the cow and "cu" means "cow" in Dutch. Dante said "cow"!'

I had missed my son's first word and I was incapable of rejoicing. In fact, I was extremely annoyed that Dante's first word had not been in Italian. I felt like an idiot and tried to share Harold's joy. Naturally, I was happy that Dante had started speaking, that was the most important thing. After a couple of minutes, however, I found myself thinking:
'Why didn't he say his first word in Italian? Does he prefer Dutch? It's because Harold never shuts up – he's always reading him books in his language... and has been ever since Dante was a week old. He's been torturing him since birth with those damned Dutch books that his grandparents buy him. This is not good. Maybe he won't speak Italian at all, only Dutch!'
I knelt down by Dante and tried talking to him slowly and clearly in Italian, using simple words in the hope that he might reproduce one. Dante looked into my eyes, smiled and repeated
'Cu, cu, cu.'
Harold was in seventh heaven. He hugged Dante and danced around with him in his arms. I pretended to be happy, but inside I felt a deep sense of failure. Some weeks would pass before, to my immense relief, Dante said his first Italian words. At last!

At 18 months, my son spoke Dutch much better than I did after months of private lessons and diligent study. I had not made the progress I had hoped for and even now when I speak Dutch, Dante actually laughs.
The thing was, I couldn't *not* learn Dutch. My husband spoke very good Italian before we had even been going out together for a year, and although at first I refused to speak Dutch – it's a difficult, ugly language and everyone in Holland speaks English anyway – I changed my mind when Dante was just a few days old and Harold started speaking Dutch to him. I wanted to know exactly what he

was saying to our tiny first-born. Usually I couldn't understand anything at all, but that day I listened very carefully. Harold was showing the little mite where Holland was on the map of Europe. Poor child! His father was in full flow:

'See, Dante, Daddy's from Amsterdam, right here in the middle of Europe. In just two hours you can be in Paris or Brussels. And Mummy's from Bari, somewhere down there between Africa and Albania, too far from Europe for anyone to bother about.'

Harold was probably joking but I had a real go at him anyway, perhaps because my hormones were still in post-natal turmoil. The following day I started an intensive Dutch course; I wasn't going to let Harold get away with teaching Dante all sorts of nonsense just because his mother didn't understand his father's language.

As I mentioned, Harold picked up Italian very quickly and even knows a few expressions in the Bari dialect. On occasions, however, he doesn't get quite the right word. I remember once in early summer, on a beach, he burned his back quite badly. Turning to my cousin Sonia, he exclaimed:

'Have you seen how red my sack is?'

Harold's most sensational linguistic gaffe, however, was during a conversation with my grandfather Vittorio, who is known to everyone as Don Vittorio. The formidable Don Vittorio is a stern man in his eighties, an old-fashioned head of family, used to being treated by all of his grandchildren with the utmost respect. The whole family was gathered round the table, eating and chatting, when Harold suddenly turned to my grandfather and said:

'Vittorio, don't talk bollocks.'

In just four words he had made three serious mistakes:
1) using the imperative when addressing my grandfather;
2) using a swear word;
3) calling my grandfather's judgment into question.

For a moment there was a deathly hush, and then I burst out laughing. A few seconds later everyone was laughing, even Don Vittorio. My mother blamed me for teaching colourful language to my husband without explaining when to use it.

After a Year and a Half in Geneva...

Dante was three and it was time for us to find a nursery for him. We had to decide what kind of place to send him to. Cleancorp payed for my children to go to the International School, but I was not convinced that this was right for Dante. I was of the opinion that a local state school would help him integrate better and grow up "normally", like me. People had told me that you get very rich, spoiled children at these private international schools. I believe that in school – as in life – you should get to know and learn to deal with people from all social backgrounds, otherwise you risk ending up with a distorted view of reality. I have heard many other people express the same opinion.

Undeniable as all this might be, the "Ecole Internationale le Mignon" private international school was extremely close to where we lived and my Tunisian and Thai neighbours were both very enthusiastic about it. Their children spoke perfect French and English without any trace of an accent. On top of which, state school lessons finish at eleven thirty a.m., a disastrous state of affairs if you are a working mother – even if I could not yet be described as such.

By this time Dante was speaking Italian and Dutch fairly well and I was wary of the idea of him having to deal with another two languages, English and French. He was only three and he would find himself speaking four languages. No, it was too much, it was ridiculous. He would just get very confused.
I read up some more on multilingual children and talked with the director of the Ecole le Mignon. The head, who had over 25 years of experience, assured me that the school was full of children who spoke four languages fluently and that this caused them no problems at all. In fact, he went on, children under six have a remarkable

ability to learn languages. I found him very convincing and felt reassured. Mindful of my own struggles to learn a foreign language, I reflected that my children were lucky to be able to attend such a school.

I decided to do the guided tour of the international school. This involved a long day observing the children in various bilingual – English and French – classes. They explained the school's methods to me and pointed out that there were fifteen children to a class, as opposed to over twenty per class in state schools. I watched the children playing happily and tried to imagine Dante there with them. I started thinking too about how enormously expensive the Ecole le Mignon was and how, if so many families were prepared to shell out so much money to send their children there, it was probably a very good school. In short, there were two possible ways of looking at it:
1) It was, in fact, an excellent school, which explained why the parents paid such high fees for their children's education;
2) It was an awful school and the parents were crazy spendthrifts who enjoyed throwing money down the drain.
Common sense told me that the first interpretation was the correct one. It was also worth remembering that we could never have afforded to pay such expensive fees ourselves. We decided to take advantage of the opportunity Cleancorp were giving us and enrol Dante in the Ecole Internationale le Mignon.

I could never have imagined how big an influence this decision would have on the future lives of all our family.

Ecole Internationale Le Mignon is a very beautiful school, along the lines of an American campus, with grass and trees and parkland; it is large but not so large as to be overwhelming for the children, whose ages range from three to eighteen years. Dante's teacher always spoke in both French and English to all the children.
'Tu dois faire pipi? Do you need to have a wee wee?'

This goes for everything: whether asking a question or telling a story, the bilingual teachers always translate.

My son quickly became best friends with an Italian boy, Lorenzo, and a Dutch boy, Alexander. I don't think this was a coincidence. This way he could speak his "mother tongues". A few months later Dante made two more great friends: Gabriel and Adrian. Gabriel spoke Chinese with his Taiwanese mother and French with his father. Adrian spoke Russian with his mother and German with his father. These children were only three but completely unfazed by all these languages, and after just a few months my son was happily playing and chattering with them in French. It was incredible – they were only three years old!

As he played, Dante switched languages. He spoke to Lorenzo in Italian and a moment later said something to Gabriel in French. It was like watching a tiny interpreter: he was accurate and effortless. I was astonished at the ease with which these children switched from one language to another.

Their body language was hilarious. When Dante spoke in Italian he waved his hands around, when he spoke French he stayed still. In fact all these children were perfectly reproducing not only the sounds of the different languages but also the accompanying gestures. Dante's French was perfect, right down to his soft pronunciation of the 'r'. There was no trace of a foreign accent; he spoke it as if it were his mother tongue. I couldn't even begin to imitate him. I speak French with a very strong accent. Before the first words are even out of my mouth people ask:

'Madame, are you Italian by any chance?'

So, after years of study, courses abroad and seven years working in Brussels, there I was speaking French with an unmistakeably Italian accent, while my son, after six months of school in Geneva and a grand total of three years of life, spoke French so perfectly that he often ended up correcting me!

This was a whole new and astonishing world for me. I studied in a state school where the only translation was from Italian into Barese dialect and vice versa. The other mothers seemed more used to it. Many of them had been to similar schools themselves or had grown up with parents from different cultural backgrounds. I, on the other hand, have a mother from Taranto and a father from Bari, so my exotic roots are limited to Puglia.

The real attraction of the Ecole le Mignon are the mothers. They fall into three categories:

VIP Mothers. With their Porsches, Bentleys, Range Rovers and limousines, they are quite a distinct species. The man accompanying them is usually the chauffeur. Welcome to the world of the indisputably rich; a world completely unknown to me!

These mothers are usually chic, gorgeous, extremely slim and kitted out in the latest fashions. They always use the earphone when talking on their mobiles. You see them happily sauntering into the school grounds with their big designer sunglasses, showing off their brilliant white teeth as they smile. They don't have the tired look of mothers who have been up all night attempting to deal with their child's violent diarrhoea or who are simply worn out by the whole exhausting process of bringing up children.

At eight in the morning their clothes and make-up are as perfect as if they were emerging from a beauty salon. What on earth time do they get up in order to look this good at 8 a.m.? I arrive feeling shattered, stressed out and usually wearing a tracksuit so as to save time and avoid being reprimanded by my son's teacher for dropping him off late. *VIP mothers* are never late, don't suffer from stress, and never run or shout at their offspring. Even if they have three, four or five children, they are always slim.

Mothers from Diplomatic Families These are multilingual, highly intelligent, cultivated, sociable women who have lived in very different countries and for whom cultural diversity has always been a way of life. Some work for the Diplomatic Corps themselves, others are accompanying their diplomat husbands around the world. Either way, they are pleasant, interesting women.

Their car number plates are marked "CD" (Corps Diplomatique) and their only problem is that they don't know how to drive. Even the simplest manoeuvres are almost beyond them and the other mothers line up to watch in disbelief as they try to turn round. Harold, who is of the firm belief that these women should not be allowed near a car, maintains that the "CD" on the number plate stands for "Cannot Drive".

On the plus side, these mothers do appear to belong to the human race: they put on weight when they get pregnant, they arrive late, they shout at their children and they are not always dressed in the latest fashions.

Mothers Who Just Happen to Be Here This is the category to which I myself belong, and in fact there can be no disputing that I just happen to find myself here. Perhaps because they are unfamiliar with the methodologies used in international schools all over the world, these mothers are astonished at the fact that their children can speak a number of foreign languages. Most significantly, they are mothers who would never be able to pay out of their own pockets for their children to go to such an expensive school.

I might be seen as a rather unedifying example of this kind of mother. In the mornings I often accompany Dante to school. I am not a morning person and my son takes after me. It takes at least thirty-five minutes to get it into his head that morning has actually arrived. After a phase of gentle coaxing, I have to resort to threats to wake him up.

We finally make it to school in my trusty blue second-hand Nissan Micra that I bought in Brussels years ago. I park between a Volvo SUV and a Range Rover. After I have taken Dante into the classroom, I always have problems finding my car on account of its being impossible to see behind the enormous vehicles of the VIP mothers.

I am always scruffily dressed; Alice, still in her pyjamas, is asleep in my arms. I am shouting at Dante and trying to catch him before he runs out into the traffic, when Alice suddenly wakes up and starts crying because she is hungry. In the rush I invariably forget to bring her bottle, so I try in vain to console her. The car journey to Dante's school takes ten very stressful minutes and when we get there the other mothers always ask me:
'Is Alice still in her pyjamas?'
I smile politely and say nothing. I am tempted to reply that it is a miracle I am not still in pyjamas myself.

John

Like some kind of desperate housewife, I head out every day with Alice to pick Dante up from school. I have always been a very sociable person and I always stop and chat at the school gate with the other mothers and, very occasionally, with the fathers. Recently I met John, a pleasant American father. A good-looking man, muscular and athletic, he turns up at school casually dressed, wearing dark sunglasses and with an air of mystery. He is not a great socialiser but he is courteous.

I am known for my ability to get conversation out of a stone and so I ended up chatting with John. One day I noticed that he had a gun – a pistol – in his trouser pocket. I wasn't particularly surprised and put it down to his perhaps being a plain-clothes policeman. Some time later I met him at a birthday party and asked him:

'John, which one is your child?'

To my great surprise, he replied:

'I don't have any children.'

Unfortunately I am not at all discreet and, besides, I am curious and tend to say what I am thinking, so I asked him:

'How is that I always see you outside school? I thought you were there to pick someone up.'

'I am. I come to pick up David. I work for his family.'

Undaunted, I pressed on:

'Are you his driver?'

'No.'

I was not about to give up, especially now that my curiosity was aroused:

'So you're a babysitter?'

'No.'

I was getting nowhere and John clearly had no desire to pursue the subject but, stubborn as a mule and without the slightest embarrassment, I asked him straight out:

'So what do you do for David's family?'

Worn down by my third degree questioning, John gave up and admitted:

'I am David's bodyguard.'

Naturally, I was unable to hide my usual gormless expression. I didn't know who David was, but I had always thought that only stars like Tom Cruise, Angelina Jolie and Michael Jackson needed bodyguards. Why would a three-year-old child at my son's school need one? I felt a sudden sense of panic... Did this mean that kidnapping children was common practice in Switzerland? Surely not. I had never heard of anything like that happening. Perhaps David's family was so rich that he was a potential target for criminals.

While I was deep in absurd thought, I saw David handing John his sweater. He was a good-looking child with blond hair and blue eyes, not unlike Dante. My sense of panic returned. What if the kidnappers got the wrong child and made off with my son instead of David? I felt uneasy at the idea of him being in a school full of rich blond kids with bodyguards. It was hard enough paying the bills each month without having kidnappers looking for ransoms. They'd never believe we lived in the villa with trains at the bottom of the garden.

Fortunately, John had noticed the look somewhere between consternation and desperation on my face, and interrupted my brooding:

'Are you feeling okay?'

My reply was perhaps the worst attempt at a joke I had ever made, but I was overwhelmed by terrifying thoughts. With a familiarity for which there was no basis whatsoever, I blurted:

'Do you know, with your dark glasses, air of mystery and super-muscular physique, you look just like James Bond: 007, licenced to kill.'

I found myself laughing alone at my own highly inappropriate joke. John became suddenly serious and looked highly offended.

Evidently he did not appreciate my sense of humour. I attempted to rectify matters:

'It was just a joke. I was joking, obviously.'

John left with David shortly afterwards and ever since he has been decidedly cold towards me. When I meet him at school I can't help thinking about my stupid joke.

Abdullah

A few months after starting school, Dante became close friends with a sweet-natured Arab boy from Bahrain, Abdullah. He arrived at school every morning in a black limousine. Next to him on the back seat there were always two women with veils. Every day it was the same routine: the smartly-dressed chauffeur parked the car, picked Abdullah up and carried him to the classroom. In fact, he always arrived wearing slippers, which was why the chauffeur wouldn't let him walk.

Right from the start I was curious about this child's background, particularly this thing about not letting his feet touch the ground. He looked like a tiny prince, and there was something compelling about the sight of him emerging from the limousine. Dante was very keen for me to invite him to play at our house, so one day I went up to the chauffeur and spoke to him in English:

'My son Dante and Abdullah are good friends and I would like to invite him to our house one afternoon next week.'

'It's not up to me to decide. I'm just the chauffeur. Could you write a note with the day and time when you want to invite him?'

It seemed a very formal way of going about things. All I wanted was to invite the child to play with Dante one afternoon. However, it is important to respect other cultures, and to see my son happy I will always do whatever it takes. I rooted in my bag for a piece of paper but all I could find was an old receipt. On the back of it I wrote:

'For Abdullah's Mother. I would like to invite your son to our house one afternoon to play with my son Dante. Below is our telephone number and address.'

The weeks passed but Abdullah's mother never phoned. One day I ran into the chauffeur as he was carrying the child into school, and I asked him about it:

'I gave you an invitation note for Abdullah's mother, but she hasn't replied. Did you give her the note?'

'You never gave *me* any note. You must have given it to my colleague Mohamed. I'm the chauffeur for Abdullah's older brother and it's purely by chance that I'm here today. The family has ten children coming to this school and there are a lot of us working for them. We've never actually seen Abdullah's mother in person. We usually just get to speak to the butler, and he will definitely have received your invitation. Mohamed will be here to pick up the child tomorrow, so you can ask him yourself. If you want to give me another invitation, I'll make sure the butler gets it.'

Once again I was left standing there with my typical gormless expression on my face. I got a grip of myself, smiled and said:

'Don't worry, it doesn't matter. It just would have been nice for my son to be able play with Abdullah.'

What I was actually thinking was: how much does this school cost Abdullah's father? With what you spend in just a year on sending ten children to the Ecole Internationale le Mignon, you could buy an apartment in Geneva. And how many chauffeurs have they got? It's going to be too much trouble to invite this child to our house to play. I'll bet his playroom is bigger than our whole house.

I didn't bother sending another invitation.

Emilie

I get on very well with a lot of Dante's classmates' mothers. Like me, most of them don't have a job. I enjoy stopping to chat with them in the school grounds. Six months after Dante started school, Emilie, one of the mothers, invited us to lunch at her house. Emilie is English, extremely pleasant and sociable. I had her down as one of the *"Mothers Who Just Happen to Be Here"*. She always turned up at school in jeans and a t-shirt and she was a good laugh. We would run into each other every day while we were waiting for the children. One day she asked:

'Do you fancy bringing Dante to lunch at my place next Wednesday? Eight of the other mothers are coming with their children. Are you free?'

'Sure, we'd love to come. Do you want me to bring something? It's a lot of work on your own – cooking for all those people. And you've got three kids! You're very brave!'

'No problem, it's just going to be a very simple lunch. But I do love Italian food, so if you want to bring something along…'

I felt sorry for Emilie: cooking for twenty people when you have three children under your feet is far from easy. I decided to whip up a splendid *pasta al forno*, using my grandmother's traditional recipe. To keep it from going cold, and also to be able to carry it without burning myself, I wrapped it in tea towels. I picked up Dante from school – he was happy and excited at the prospect of having lunch with his new friends – and we set off in convoy, following Emilie to her house.

I have always hated this way of doing things because I often end up getting lost. As I followed the convoy of cars (undoubtedly all belonging to *VIP mothers*), I realised that my blue Micra was the smallest of the lot.

We arrived at a large iron gate and Emilie rather ostentatiously took a large remote control from the dashboard and opened it. For about a hundred metres we followed a driveway set amid immaculate lawns and parked on a spacious gravel clearing in front of an enormous colonnade. We got out of the car and I realised, on closer inspection, that the villa was an old 18th century house resting in the shade of huge hundred-year-old trees. I imagined it was one of those old mansions that has been converted into luxury apartments and looked around for the entrance, idly wondering which floor Emilie lived on.

'Have you seen? What a fantastic castle!'

The voice belonged to Nathalie, a Canadian mother who had been living in Geneva for some years. Clutching my *pasta al forno* still wrapped in its tea towels, I looked at her in surprise. Dante was excitedly pushing me in the direction of his friends. For the first time in my life I was about to go into a castle and have lunch with its owner. It was simply enormous, far too big for a single family. I looked at Nathalie and whispered:

'Surely it's not just her family living in a castle this big?'

At the top of her voice – unfortunately Canadians are not famous for being discreet – Nathalie bellowed:

'Of course not. All her staff live here too.'

We were now at the entrance to the castle and I was starting to feel embarrassed about my *pasta al forno* wrapped in tea towels. I had thought it was going to be an informal lunch with a few of the other mothers. I wasn't as casually dressed as usual but if I had known, I would certainly have made more effort.

Who would have thought that Emilie lived in a castle? The door was opened by an elegantly-dressed elderly lady who I supposed was Emilie's mother. I felt as though I ought to shake her hand and introduce myself as a friend of her daughter's. She spoke to me in French, with a Brazilian accent, and led us into an immense drawing room. Almost all of the other mothers were already there. I saw Emilie and, somewhat embarrassed, handed her the dish of *pasta al forno*.

Emilie said:

'Thank you. What a treat to have some real Italian pasta! Even if today we're going to be eating Brazilian. I want to see how good my new cook really is.'

I must have had one of my famous gormless expressions on my face. I collected myself and remarked:

'I love Brazilian food. It's one of my favourite types of cuisine.'

It wasn't true. I had eaten Brazilian only once in my life, at least ten years before. To be honest, I couldn't even name a Brazilian dish. And to think I'd been worrying about poor Emilie slaving over the stove with her three children under her feet. It had taken me all morning to cook the meatballs and special tomato sauce needed for my grandmother's *pasta al forno* recipe, and here I was at lunch in a castle where there were not only staff waiting on us at table but also a Brazilian cook!

Emilie was wearing tattered Levis and no shoes and her big toe was peeping through a hole in one of her white tennis socks; you could see part of her toe-nail. Appearances are deceptive, but there could be no doubting that this was the house of a *VIP Mother*.

We mothers lunched in a spacious dining room while our children were waited on in the kitchen by the staff. After lunch a babysitter was assigned to keep the children entertained in a playroom upstairs. After a few minutes I recognised the sound of Dante's desperate crying. I found him on the stairs and he confided:

'I went to the toilet for a pee and I got lost. I can't find the playroom with all my friends.'

I assured him we would find them but then we both got lost and it was only after wandering around for a while that we came upon the room where his friends were.

The lunch was very pleasant and I had a good time, but I realised that I was in a world I didn't belong to. I was curious to observe the *VIP Mothers*. At one point, Salma, a beautiful Lebanese mother said:

'I brought some typical Lebanese food. Try some. It's exquisite.'

I tasted it and it was excellent. I asked her for the recipe for her exceptionally delicious meatballs, and she replied:

'I didn't cook any of it myself. We ordered it from 'Leha', a Lebanese restaurant near where we live. We have a year-round arrangement with them: they prepare and deliver our dinner every evening. It's my husband's favourite restaurant.'

Emilie added:

'I love that restaurant; it's the best Lebanese restaurant in Geneva.'

I did some brief sums in my head. In Geneva all restaurants, without exception, are expensive. I didn't even want to imagine how dear the best Lebanese restaurant in the whole city might be. This woman ordered dinner from this place every single evening, and even had it delivered to the door. She had four children, a husband, a mother-in-law and a live-in maid. How much did she spend in a year on family dinners? There could be no doubt about Salma's status as a *VIP Mother*.

That evening I excitedly recounted our adventure to Harold. He listened in amusement and then, with the engineer's eye for the practical, asked:

'Wouldn't it be worth Salma's husband paying for her to do a Lebanese cooking course? He'd save a load of money!'

Mattias' Birthday

Harold hadn't yet realised that Salma's husband was not the slightest bit bothered about how much the restaurant cost, also because their family undoubtedly lived in the same unrestrained luxury as Emilie's. Harold still hadn't realised what kind of world our son's schoolmates lived in.

One day we received an invitation to a birthday party for one of Dante's friends, Mattias, and my husband decided to come with us. We were on the chemin du Lac looking for Mattias' house when eventually we arrived in front of an enormous, splendid villa high above the lake. Harold was convinced that the address on the invitation must have been wrong. I disagreed – partly because I knew what the world of *VIP Mothers* looked like, partly because on the gate I could see balloons and the words "HAPPY BIRTHDAY, MATTIAS".

Faced with the evidence, Harold had to admit I was right. We rang and, as the gate opened automatically, a recorded voice announced: 'Welcome to the Villa Lauriane.'

I burst out laughing but Harold told me off, pointing out that there were closed circuit TV cameras everywhere and that I was going to embarrass us. I quickly pulled myself together as a man in a jacket and tie motioned to us to stop. He asked for our names and surnames and checked his list before letting us through another gate. We then drove through parkland for several hundred metres and, being an anxious mother, I couldn't help but imagine little Mattias getting lost in all the trees. Before long, however, the sheer beauty of the colours of the leaves made me forget my worries. It was a gloriously sunny day and I felt like I was in a film. We finally reached the car park, next to which the children spotted an ostrich farm. They had ostriches here?

Another man in a jacket and tie showed us where to park, opened the car door for me and gave me his hand to help me out. I was back in that film again. The smartly-dressed man led the way and the four of us followed. We proceeded to the front door of the villa where a liveried housekeeper let us in. We said hello and handed her Mattias' present, which she placed in a large basket full of wrapped gifts.

The house was beautiful: modern, colourful and full of fantastic paintings. It had one particularly striking – if at first disconcerting – feature: a transparent floor. You could see into the rooms above and below and the effect was rather dizzying. Dante and Alice stood stock still, paralysed with fear of falling through the floor. Harold and I could see that our children were not going to be receptive to explanations about the aesthetic principles of modern architecture, and we both burst out laughing. We tried to convince them that it was okay to walk around, but they were having none of it. Alice started screaming and crying, attracting the curious attention of the other guests.

With great delicacy, the lady of the house came to our rescue. At the school occasionally I had already caught glimpses of Lauriane, a gorgeous Frenchwoman always dressed very fashionably. I had already chalked her down as a *VIP Mother* but, from that day on, she was for me the undisputed leader of the gang. Harold and I picked up the children and apologised to Lauriane.

The party was a triumph, perfectly organised down to every last detail. There were about twenty entertainers and around fifty children with their parents. On arrival, each child received a gift of an Adidas swimming costume and matching towel. After getting the children into their swimming costumes, we made our way into a large pink and turquoise room, next to the living room. It contained a beautiful green swimming pool. The children and entertainers all dived in and clambered onto little coloured, duck-shaped boats. The children then got back out of the pool, plunged happily into a tub of coloured soap and, covered in suds, jumped back into the water. An entertainer dressed as a pirate sang and got the guests dancing, a clown performed conjuring tricks and someone dressed in a Winnie the Pooh outfit helped the children to do hand paintings on enormous sheets of paper. There was also a teenager dressed as a princess, putting make-up on the little guests. In a large adjacent room there were two buffets, one for the children and one for the adults, which included dishes from all over the world. I grabbed a huge piece of steaming hot focaccia; it looked just like the focaccia we have in Bari. I complimented Lauriane on how good it was and she explained:

'I'm really glad you like it. Our assistant cook is from Naples.'

I complimented her on her choice of staff too, and immediately felt ridiculous. Was I really congratulating someone for having the good taste to employ a Neapolitan in her kitchen? It was perhaps simply a way of concealing my surprise that she had at least two people helping out just with the cooking.

For us, paying a baby-sitter was enough of a struggle. Our worlds were so far apart that Harold and I actually began to feel embarrassed at finding ourselves at such a party. We tried not to let it show and pretended to be completely at ease. Dante and Alice were happy as could be and were having a great time with their friends.

It was time for the cake – a chocolate cake about two metres by five, in the shape of a larger-than-life-sized car. It was covered in white chocolate and meringue, and HAPPY BIRTHDAY, MATTIAS was written on it in glistening letters. Unfortunately, Mattias was nowhere to be seen. His baby-sitters – both the English-speaking one and the French-speaking one – were searching frantically for him.

It turned out he had got bored with the festivities and was running on one of his father's exercise machines near the swimming pool changing rooms. He was going so fast that it took the French babysitter some time to catch him.

Eventually, Mattias was brought in to see his cake. I, for one, couldn't take my eyes off it: in all my life I had never seen such a big and beautiful cake. Not even at the most over-the-top weddings in the south of Italy would you ever see such a thing. I saw that both my children were gazing open-mouthed at the enormous mass of chocolate in front of them. I nonchalantly strolled over to them and discreetly closed their gaping mouths.

When the party was over, Lauriane gave my children beautiful presents from the Disney Shop in Paris. These gifts had almost certainly cost more than the one we had given Mattias.

Back in our villa with the railway line running through the garden, Harold and I couldn't stop talking about the party. Harold asked me: 'Is everybody in this country stinking rich?'

'Apparently. I read in a local magazine that 7% of the population of Switzerland are millionaires – that's one out of every 14 people. Just imagine! This year alone they have let in over 900 new people who are worth over 10 million Swiss Francs each. It's all the tax incentives they offer here. If you're really and truly rich, this is the place you want to be. If we were millionaires, do you think we would do the same?'

'I don't know... but... I don't think so. Do the kids of these millionaires all go to school at le Mignon?'

'Not all... but I rather suspect that the *VIP Mothers* outnumber the *"Mothers Who Just Happen to Be Here"*.'

I felt privileged to have had the opportunity to mingle with this "other world".

The University

After two years in Geneva

At this point, I hadn't worked for two years; looking after the children was a full-time job. It was a wonderful, unique and remarkable experience and I count myself lucky to have had the privilege. But what happens to a reasonably intelligent, cultivated woman who for two consecutive years devotes herself exclusively to bringing up her children?

Gradually – and irreversibly – your brain cells begin to burn out. Once this process starts, urgent action is needed, but at first you don't realise what is happening. There are no obvious symptoms. And then one day you find yourself:

- frantically collecting loyalty card points in five different local supermarkets;
- watching any and every reality show on any and every TV channel;
- devouring and remembering the sordid details of the stories in the gossip columns;
- cutting out and saving recipes of every kind;
- spending days on end pondering the choice of entertainer for your children's next birthday party.

You begin to become obsessed about things which are really not so important at all. You find yourself talking with other mothers about laundry, chicken pox, dysentery and cream for babies' red bottoms. You start getting excited about a new fabric conditioner or the wedding of some TV celebrity.

How can you tell when the gradual process of brain cell burn-out has begun? It's a difficult thing to do on your own. You need someone to point out with delicacy and sensitivity that your intellectual powers are on the wane.

In my case that someone was Harold. One evening we were watching the reality show: *Celebrity Survivor*. Harold can't stand the programme and calls it *Pathetic Survivor*. I was close to tears because one of the people involved was reading out a letter from her son.

Harold was looking at me with an expression of disbelief:

'You are definitely going soft in the head. What's happening to you? You need to get back to work as soon as possible.'

He was brief and to the point. He didn't really need to say anything else. In just a few words he'd summed up exactly what the problem was. I didn't get angry, hysterical or aggressive. He was right, and deep down I knew it.

Looking for Work

That was how I started looking for a job. I updated my CV, even though there wasn't much to add as I hadn't been working. I sent off about fifty CVs to the legal departments of banks, private companies and international organisations. In the south of Italy we are used to unemployment and to the realities of looking for work. As a result we are flexible, prepared to compromise and don't have very high expectations. I tried everything. I didn't get a single interview. They all replied – every last one of them – professionally and politely. The gist of their letters was:

'We read your CV with interest. We are sorry to inform you, however, that you do not fit the profile of candidate we are looking for. Yours sincerely…'

The strange thing is, though, that in Switzerland there is hardly any unemployment at all!

It's true that my first degree thesis was on European Union law, that my post-graduate degree was on European Union law and that during my seven years in Brussels I worked in areas related to European Union law. In short, my specialist field was European Law!

Switzerland is not and probably never will be part of the European Union, so why should employers here be interested in my CV? To get an idea, you just have to take a look at one of the fliers that regularly find their way into your letterbox.

I still remember the leaflets they were handing out at the time of the referendum on whether or not Switzerland should sign up to the Schengen Accord. There was one guy going around screaming in terror about what a disaster it would be to go along with the agreement. He predicted a 21st century Hun invasion of the country. Criminals, low-lifes, convicts on leave from prison and dangerous individuals of every shape and form would pour into Switzerland from the various European Union countries, bringing with them theft, murder, gun-fights and Mafia-like associations. Our lives would all be in constant danger and it would be like living in Baghdad. In short, the Swiss are not exactly ardent pro-Europeans. They might better be described as enthusiastic nationalists. In other words, I was in the wrong country with the wrong CV.

I identified three possible solutions to the problem of finding a job:
1. persuade the citizens of the Swiss Confederation to join the European Union;
2. persuade Swiss human resources managers that my specialist knowledge of European Union law was actually of great value to them;
3. go back to studying.

Of these three options, the third struck me immediately as being the least realistic. It often happens in life, however, that the least attractive alternative becomes the only possible way forward. But at 34 years of age, with two young children to look after, was I seriously contemplating the idea of going back to my studies? No...

The Master's Degree

What I really wanted was to work in the legal department of a bank, private company or international organisation somewhere... anywhere.

I did some background research and the best option appeared to be a Master's degree for law students organised by the University of Geneva and funded by a group of Swiss banks and private companies. To my delight and surprise I was selected along with 24 other Swiss and foreign law students. In order to do the Master's I had to enrol at the university and this involved bringing a series of documents to the Admissions Office.

A week after I had done this, I received a letter informing me that the University was not accepting my enrolment application because I had not submitted the original of my school exam certificate. I went to speak with the secretary in the Admissions Office and asked:

'But if you have my original degree certificate, why would you need more than a copy of my school exam certificate? If I have a degree, then it stands to reason that I must have gone to school and passed my school-leaving exams. Otherwise I could never have got into an Italian university in the first place.'

'If you don't bring us the original school-leaving exam certificate within two weeks, your application to enrol at this university will be rejected and you won't be able to attend the Master's course.'

The secretary was unmoved. Absurdly and pointlessly inflexible. I muttered something about hoping I would be able to find the original of the document they wanted. As I was leaving, a thin blond girl with rather intense eyes came up to me. She had been behind me in the queue while I was arguing with the secretary. She smiled and consoled me:

'Don't get upset about it. I know the secretary well. He's just doing what he's been told to do, and he's not allowed to make exceptions.

He's only doing his job. I risked my life to get my original school exam certificate!

My name's Arta, by the way. I'm from Kosovo. I left there in 1998 because of the terrible war. The Albanian government gave me a grant to study at university in Switzerland. I really wanted to study law, like I was doing in Kosovo. When I tried to enrol in the Law Faculty here in Geneva, all I had was a photocopy of my school exam certificate. The secretary, the one you were just arguing with, wouldn't accept it.

I tried to get him to understand, pointed out to him about the war in Kosovo. But he was having none of it. I went back to Kosovo to get the original certificate and I was captured by Serbian paramilitaries. They kept me prisoner for five days, five long days, the worst of my life. They wanted to kill me. It's a miracle I'm here, but I am and it feels so good to be alive. I managed to escape with the documents I needed to enrol here. I graduated last year!'

Her story was so incredible that I didn't know what to say. I was amazed, dumbstruck! Not even a terrible war would soften his heart. I was surprised by how Arta just accepted this. She wasn't angry with the guy, she actually defended him. What a marvellous woman! I liked her and we ended up chatting for hours. She was sensitive, strong and determined: a real heroine for our times, the first I had ever met.

If I had been Arta, the secretary would have been my worst enemy. My hatred would have known no bounds. If the guy had been blind, I would have dumped him in the middle of the Salerno-Reggio Calabria motorway and left him to cross it on his own.

Fortunately, I managed to find the certificate I needed, without so much as being captured! It was in one of the boxes I had left years before at my parents' place in Bari.

The Master's degree was a full-time one-year course and attendance was obligatory. There were eight hours of lessons a day and four written and oral exams in the course of the year. By this time Alice, like Dante, was going to the Ecole Internationale le Mignon, and Harold had said he would give me all the help I needed. I wasn't too worried about the exams. I had never had problems at university in Italy and I was sure that, with a few sacrifices, I could make a success of it. My life was about to change, but I hadn't an inkling of just how much.

In September I started attending lessons at the University of Geneva.

The university was modern, spacious and well-organised and the lessons were held in a large room with three overhead projectors and one ordinary projector.

On the first day, the course director introduced the programme of study and spoke about how the course would be organised. He was a good-looking man of about fifty, tall, slim and blond. He was refined and witty. And wit is a quality that cannot be taken for granted – sometimes it even evokes surprise – in Switzerland.

The introductory lesson was interesting and enjoyable. It emerged that every year there were students who did not pass their exams, failed the course and therefore did not find work with one of the banks or companies that funded the Master's programme. How strange I thought: a post-graduate course where they fail people – it was a new concept for me.

The average age of the students was 26 and, at 34, I felt out of place. I had the distinct impression I was seen as a thirty-something loser who had somehow found her way into this class of very young and highly motivated recent graduates. They were all used to studying while I – for obvious reasons – was completely out of practice. And then there was my problem with burnt-out brain cells...

Places were assigned to us and I found myself sitting next to Jérôme, a pleasant-looking guy from Lausanne who had only recently graduated. He was cheerful and friendly.

There were only ten foreign students in the class; we were clearly in a minority. I couldn't help noticing two Brazilian girls, both incredibly beautiful and unassuming; they looked like models from *Vogue*. During the coffee break the guys tried to talk to them but they were very distant and unsociable. Perhaps when you are that beautiful it's the only way to deal with men hitting on you all the time.

In the first lesson on Banking Law I had problems following because the teacher kept using a French word I didn't know. I leaned over and whispered to Jérôme:
'I don't understand. What was that last word he used?'
Irritably and without so much as glancing in my direction, Jérôme cut me dead:
'Quiet. Stop bothering me.'
The lesson came to an end. After a few minutes I went up to Jérôme and said:
'French is a foreign language for me. If you had spared me just a few seconds, I would have been able to follow the whole two-hour lesson much better.'
Even more irritably than before, he replied:
'It's selfish of you to disturb me while I am listening to the teacher. If your French isn't good enough, why did you sign up for this degree? How did you manage to get in?'
I hated Jérôme, my own deskmate. I felt humiliated, especially as I was nearly ten years older than him. Young people these days had no respect for their elders. I found myself thinking like an old lady. There was no need to get carried away, though: I was only 34. I went off for a coffee with the Brazilian goddesses. Fortunately there were understanding people I could talk to.

After a few days I suddenly realised that my life had changed drastically. I was waking up very early every morning and getting the children ready for Harold to take them to school. I would then go out into the garden and catch the train to university.

Swiss trains are extremely punctual. If they are so much as a minute late, everyone gets very annoyed and complains bitterly. A mortified voice then embarrassedly apologises for the terrible delay. My relationship with time and punctuality had improved, but the mornings were a real rush. I always ended up dashing out into the garden and diving onto the train at the last minute. I was terrified of missing it.

Once on the train, I would finish getting dressed and putting my make-up on. The other commuters would look on in astonishment as I tied my shoe laces and combed my hair. In the evenings I would get home shattered after the course. It was a real struggle for me to follow all those lessons in English and French. I was starting to feel the effects of all the brain cells I had lost during my desperate housewife phase. It took a few weeks, in fact, for my brain to start working properly again.

After I got home I would make dinner for the children, put them to bed and study till late. At the weekends I studied for hours on end. I had never studied so much in my life. Working with the mind like that required an enormous effort, but the hope of finding a job gave me the strength to persevere. Before enrolling at the university, I had spoken with Italian students who had done the same degree in previous years and they had all found work quite easily at the end of the course. There was hope even for me!

And here I was a week into the course at my first lesson on Swiss Law. The teacher was an effeminate man of about fifty; he wasn't very tall and had a hysterical manner. Unlike the other courses, this was held in a large lecture theatre which could hold at least a hundred students. The lesson began at 9:15 and when I arrived at 9:16 the door was already closed. I went in as quietly as I could and assumed an air of mortified regret. This was supposed to serve as a discreet apology for my being late, but the teacher broke off in mid-sentence, looked at me in icy silence and announced:

'If you wish to attend my lessons, you arrive on time. Out!'

I didn't realise at first that he was talking to me. I had already taken a seat and was looking for a pen to take notes. But when I looked up from my bag, there were a hundred pairs of eyes staring at me. I heard sounds of laughter and noticed that the teacher too was staring right at me. I gasped:

'I'm sorry, were you talking to me?'

'So, not only do you arrive late and interrupt my lesson, but you don't even listen to what I say?'

Loud laughter. The students were loving it.

'I'm terribly sorry, but my train was late; that's why I only just got here.'

The train had been maybe 50 seconds late and then I hadn't been able to find the classroom. To be honest, I hadn't even realised I was late.

'You could have caught an earlier train. Please leave the classroom immediately. Latecomers are not permitted to attend my lessons.'

He was definitely making an example out of me.

The previous night I had been up till 1 a.m. studying economics. I had then got up at half past five to study some more. My husband was abroad on business. I had woken the children, washed, dressed and fed them, and taken them to school. I had then rushed home and jumped on the 8:15 train. During the journey I had read through some court rulings because the bastard who was now staring me down had gone overboard with his homework assignments. And now I was supposed to get up and leave and miss a two-hour lesson because I had arrived one minute – *one* lousy minute – late?

Everyone was still looking at me. The students were thoroughly entertained.

I tried sucking up – with bastards like this guy it sometimes works:

'Professor, forgive me, but couldn't you make an exception just this once? I very much want to follow your course.'

'I never make exceptions.'

I put all my books back in my bag and left the classroom. This teacher was a scumbag. I spent the next two hours in the university bar.

Why was there no tolerance or flexibility in this country? Why was it not possible to make exceptions?

Why was it that if I went into a restaurant with my two children starving to death and asked if they had a table they would tell me they didn't?

Why if I realised that there were two tables for two and suggested pushing them together, would the waiter tell me that it wasn't possible, that they never changed the way the tables were laid out? Waiter, why would you make me wait 45 minutes and starve my children to death because changing the layout of the tables in your restaurant is not permitted? The two tables were only fifty centimetres apart! Why was it not possible to push them together? I wasn't expecting them to behave like Italians – for us, making exceptions is the rule – but was just a smidgeon of flexibility too much to ask for?

I was depressed and demoralised. And then Sophie finished me off. At the end of the lesson I asked her:

'How was it? Interesting? Could I borrow your notes and photocopy them?'

'No, they're a mess. I can't let you have them. It was a really interesting lesson. It's a pity you missed it... How come you were late?'

I couldn't take any more of this. If you're from Bari, arriving one minute late means being ridiculously early. I had been on time, damn it! We were talking about one minute. *One* minute.

'The train was late and I have two small children.'

'There's no way you can do this Master's degree with two small children. There's too much stuff to study. How are you going to prepare the exams? You know they fail people? What did you enrol

113

for? Wouldn't you have been better off staying at home with the kids?'

I thought:

'What kind of stupid question is that? Sophie, darling, are you trying to put the hoodoo on me? I know they fail people, but why should they fail me?'

Sophie was from Geneva, twenty-five years old, a recent graduate. She was attractive – slim, blond, average height. She struck me as studious and determined. She always had something to say in the lessons.

I think the prevailing philosophy here is that mothers should stay at home, look after the house and not harbour ambitions beyond maternity. When I told my Swiss neighbours I was going to do a Master's degree, they thought I was an unnatural mother.

It was the year 2000! When were they going to get emancipated? Women didn't get the vote here till 1971. Compare that with Italy (1946), France (1944) and Great Britain (1928). In other words, women here had to wait 25 years longer than their Italian counterparts to win the right to vote, and even then they probably didn't actually ask for it. How could that happen?

In Italy the law establishing equal treatment for women and men in the workplace was passed in 1977; in Switzerland they had to wait until 1996. Nearly twenty years later.

And that's not all. A reform of Swiss family law establishing the equality of spouses was introduced in 1988. So it is only since then that women in Switzerland have had the same legal rights as their husbands. And it wasn't until 2004 that women became entitled to paid maternity leave. Before that, they had to forego their salary for the whole duration of their maternity leave. Is it a coincidence that lessons in state schools finish at 11:20 a.m.? Maybe they want to make it impossible for us to work?

A friend of mine from Rome who is married to a guy from Geneva told me that her in-laws refused to look after her children because they didn't want her to work. She kept secret the fact that she worked, so as to avoid tensions. Not even my grandmother in Taranto had to deal with that kind of problem! She was working as early as the 1940s.

I didn't reply further to Sophie. It would have involved too much explaining and I just didn't feel like it. She wound me up: how could you be so bigoted at such an early age?

The Interactive Method

The Master's degree was organised, like an MBA, using The Interactive Method. This meant that the students were encouraged to contribute at all times during lessons. In other words, if you hadn't been studying, they were going to pick up on it right away. In the middle of the lessons, without any warning and when you least expected it, the teachers would suddenly ask you a question. You couldn't therefore let your thoughts wander to how Alice was coping with her cold or what to buy for dinner or how useless the babysitter was.

Every evening we had to read and study documents on which we would be tested the following day. Unfortunately, I was not in a strategically advantageous position in the classroom: my seat was in the front row, so I was right in the teacher's line of vision every time an impossible question came up. Seating positions were assigned by the course directors. I have always hated the front row and, in fact, at school I always sat at the back of the class, at a safe distance from the teachers' enquiring eyes.

So why were they now always asking *me*? I don't know if it was because of my dreadful seating position. Perhaps because I had blurted out a completely wrong answer in one of the first lessons. Or because I was a foreigner. Or maybe because I was the only mother with two children. Or something in my eyes or facial expression suggested ignorance or worry. Whatever the reason was, I couldn't turn up unprepared because you could count on them finding me out.

My decision to adopt the Study-Every-Day methodology was the result of several embarrassing moments early in the course. When I was at university in Italy, I had always been one of those students who lock themselves in their room for a month before an exam. Lack of air and sunlight would leave my face with the same milky white hue as the walls of my room. I never left the house. I studied night and day. I had nightmares about the exam and lived in a constant state of stress and anxiety, but my powers of concentration were formidable and I could memorise anything. I avoided watching the news because I would end up memorising the things they reported on. There was no time for talking on the phone to friends. I didn't socialise. It was a case of total isolation.

Back then, outside of exam time, it was a different story: I went out every evening, had a wild time going to discos and maintained a steady stream of boyfriends. In short, I had a full and active life. The methodology was Last Minute Study. But now with the Master's degree and twenty different exam subjects to prepare, I had to change my approach and change it quickly.

During a lesson on Swiss Law, I was surprised by the teacher's tendency to idealise his own country. Italians are naturally self-critical. We spend hours of our lives criticising our country, are always finding fault with it and complain constantly.

The class was discussing banking secrecy and corruption. I asked the teacher:

'In your opinion, does banking secrecy lead to more widespread corruption?'

'There is no corruption here. We're not in Italy, Brazil or Mexico, you know.'

Although his tone was extremely courteous, he made a point of looking at me when he mentioned Italy, Erika (my Mexican friend) when he mentioned Mexico, and Camila and Anapaola (my Brazilian friends) when he said the word "Brazil". We found his comment highly offensive. The Swiss students in the class agreed with the teacher.

One of the extraordinary things about the European Union is the practice of comparing laws in the different member states with the aim of finding the best one for Community-wide application. Comparing oneself with others, questioning one's own way of doing things and discussing which approach is best is an enriching process.

After all, it is always possible that someone else will have found a better way of doing things. I am an ardent pro-European and I found myself living in a country of fervent nationalists.

To illustrate what I mean, here is the title of an article from the *Tribune de Geneve* (7th November, 2008) on an interview with Micheline Calmy Rey, the foreign minister. It concerns the bilateral accord between the European Union and Switzerland on taxation. The headline read:

'We Won't Take Lessons From Anyone.'

In Italy we are all convinced that in other countries they do things better than we do. We're often wrong. But we are unshaken in our belief that the grass is greener on the other side of the fence. In Switzerland, on the other hand, they are convinced that the grass in their garden is the greenest you can get.

Nerds – A New Breed

My classmates on the master's course were quite unlike any students I had ever met. When I was at school there were always nerds in the class. Usually they were losers, ugly, anti-social and spotty; they had thick glasses and no life. In my school there were two types: the *Solidarity Nerds* and the *Lone Nerds*.

The Solidarity Nerds.
- Would write their Latin translations on carbon paper and pass them on to the rest of the class.
- Could give you a five-minute summary of the history lesson they had spent all the previous afternoon studying.
- When you were being tested, would whisper the answers to you.
- Much loved, they could on occasions be witty and amusing.
- Their notes were freely available on request.
- They never attended lessons during student strikes, especially on Saturdays, regardless of whether the strike was justified or simply an excuse to bunk off.
- Always understanding of other students' points of view, they were happy when their classmates got good marks.

The Lone Nerds.
- Never helped you in tests.
- Never whispered an answer to you.
- Forever putting up their hands to ask or answer questions and show off how hard they had been studying, thus embarrassing those who hadn't.
- Would never give you their notes.
- During strikes would always attend lessons, even in the face of serious threats and even on Saturdays – which meant mountains of homework for the weekend.

- Utterly detested and bereft of redeeming features, they were never invited to birthday parties, for obvious reasons.
- Jealous and envious if classmates got good marks.

Most of my classmates on the Master's course fell into a new category: *Attractive Lone Nerds*. Yes, their appearance was deceptive: they were good-looking, well-dressed and had an active social life. You wouldn't have expected them to be such fine examples of *Lone Nerds*. It came as a surprise when you realised what they were actually like.

Their main hobby was raising their hand to answer a question someone else had struggled with. As a result of overdoing these "classroom gymnastics", they quickly developed juvenile arthritis and at night would fall asleep with their arms still raised. If nothing else, they were consistent: they would never whisper an answer to you and they would never lend you their notes. Ever.

Then I found Rachel. A very generous Swiss girl of 26, Rachel became my guardian angel. She belonged, without a shadow of doubt, to the category of *Solidarity Nerds*. Unselfishly, she made her notes available to the whole class, without exceptions. She was extremely bright, really knew her stuff and was always happy to explain even the most difficult concepts. Rachel would help anyone with anything at any time. At the end of the course she won the prize for Best Student and I was delighted because she really deserved it.

There wasn't any great solidarity between the students in the class, but they were frighteningly competitive. All of them – and I mean all – studied like crazy. I decided to talk to Rachel to try to find out why they wouldn't help each other, because for me this was something quite new.

Rachel explained:

'I haven't noticed anything different compared to when I was at school or doing my first degree.'

Curious as to how Swiss schools worked, I asked:

'So when you went to school there was a lot of competition between students and they all studied like crazy?'

'Yes, especially when we were about twelve. That's an important age. If you don't do well at school and you don't get into the top class, you don't get into university.'

'Sorry, let me get this clear. When the kids are twelve, the teachers decide whether they'll be good enough to go to university or not? And if you're not good enough, you'll never be able to go to university?'

'Exactly. Once they decide that you're not up to it, your school career is mapped out and you won't get into university.'

I was staggered. My brother would never have graduated if he had lived in Switzerland. When he was twelve he was one of the worst students in the class and his teachers didn't know what to do with him. My parents were far from overjoyed but they were still confident about his future. As you get older you change, you become more mature. Now my brother has a prestigious job as an engineer at the airport in Bari.

I don't think it's right what they do here; you have to give a child the chance to grow up. There's no way you can decide a kid's future when he's twelve.

Still, I was beginning to understand the *Attractive Lone Nerds* better. They had no choice. From an early age, kids here are used to fighting tooth and nail, sweating blood, just to get through school. Not hard then to see why adults on a university post-graduate course would behave the way they did. I was suddenly seeing my classmates in a new light.

I had been lucky enough to make friends with a group of foreign girls who were pretty much in the same boat as me. There was no rivalry between us; we helped each other a lot and all we wanted was to successfully complete the Master's course together.

Anapaola had just moved from Brazil to Geneva to be with her husband. She was reserved and kept everyone, apart from us girlfriends, at a distance. Like the rest of our little group, she did not feel on the same wavelength as the other students on the course.

Then one day my witty desk-mate Jérôme, piped up with:

'How can you people stand it in Brazil? What a ridiculous country – they don't even stop at red lights. I mean, do you even have laws down there in the Third World? I've never been but… I've heard lots of strange things about it…'

Up to that point Anapaola had never lost her composure and had always been completely unruffled. But this time you could see in her eyes that she was extremely pissed off.

She stared back at Jérôme and said:

'I would advise you never to come to Brazil because you would never get out alive!'

Good on you, girl! I couldn't stop laughing for twenty minutes. Jérôme's expression of dumbstruck disbelief was a picture. He hadn't bargained for that kind of response – especially from someone as polite, reserved and discreet as Anapaola.

"Banking Secrecy" at the University

Everyone knows that Swiss law ensures banking secrecy. Banks are obliged to guarantee maximum protection of client information. Violation of banking secrecy is punishable with a heavy fine or a jail sentence. As a result of this, banking secrecy is respected. With regard to the Master's course, there are secrets which are respected by the administration and teaching staff with the same seriousness and rigour as applies to banking secrets. And yet, in the event of these secrets being violated, there is no heavy fine or jail sentence. Rigour, inflexibility and absolute seriousness are the order of the day.

The Master's degree teaching staff is made up of exceptional teachers, fine professionals who believe completely in the value of the course. Some years earlier, these same highly qualified and talented teachers must have met to decide on the methodology they would use for the Master's. It would undoubtedly have been a cold, wet, misty winter afternoon: one of those days in which everyone is in a bad mood.

One of them must have put forward a question such as:

'How can we get our students to study thirteen subjects, 24 hours a day, like sleepless lunatics, but then give them exams on only three or four subjects? Setting exams in all the subjects would just be too complicated. And we need to be sure they know all the subjects inside-out, otherwise they won't have earned their diploma.'

A professor in a very bad mood – the type of guy with some serious personal problem, who's undergoing an existential crisis, who has been depressed for ever and is wickeder than Snow White's wicked witch, more cynical than Cinderella's step-mother – had an evil, sadistic idea something along the lines of:

'Here's a great way we can solve the problem and get them to study like crazy, as well as stressing the hell out of them. They'll be anguished, desperate and dead on their feet but they'll really know their stuff! We won't let them know what subjects the exams are going to be on until the day before. That way they'll have to study everything. There's no way you can prepare two, three or four exams in a few hours, so if they've studied all the subjects they'll pass, otherwise they'll fail!'

So it was that at 5 p.m. on the day before the exam, a terrifying email announcing the exam subjects for the following morning was sent to all the students on the course. The wait was stressful and exhausting. Every minute was precious. We were all glued to our computers, staring at our mailboxes, willing the message to arrive.

It was 4:59 p.m. and I was in a state of great agitation. I was twitching, suffering from panic attacks and what might be asthma attacks too. I looked anxiously at the computer to see if the email had arrived. And suddenly there it was!

I was scared to open it. Couldn't the bastards have sent it earlier? Even at 4 p.m., just to give us an extra hour to revise. Every minute was precious. But even in this case they were punctual beyond belief. The email did not arrive so much as a second before 5 p.m. I opened the damned thing at least four times. There was just one simple sentence telling me which subjects I would be tested on the following morning. I was paralysed with terror. I clicked again and re-opened the message. I was incapable of either reading or understanding. Finally I calmed down and tried to reassure myself. I took a deep breath. There were almost tears in my eyes but I didn't cry – there was no point. I read the thing properly and took in what was written. I would never have expected this: what on earth were these subjects they had chosen? There were only a few hours to work on them – the subjects you hated most, the ones you had studied least; or the ones with the shittiest teachers on the Master's course. It was going to be a long night.

The strategies that we, like the students before us, employed to discover what the exam topics were, included:

- in-depth statistical analysis of the subjects that had come up in the previous five years;
- cunning questions to the teachers regarding their trips abroad;
- trying to bribe the Nigerian secretary, Minga, whose job it was to send the terrifying email.

So far none of these strategies had ever worked and the subjects that had come up had always been the least expected ones.

Minga, professional and devoted to duty, was incorruptible. My Brazilian girlfriends and I had tried everything but it was no use. Minga was a lawyer as well as the assistant to a professor at the University. He was a graduate of the Master's programme who had never found a job as a lawyer in Geneva. He seemed to me to really know his stuff. One day I questioned him:

'How come you never tried to get work in a bank or a multinational – something outside the University?'

'Believe me, I tried. Geneva is an intolerant city with problems of racism. I have excellent references and a good CV but I've never been able to find a job outside the University.'

'I'm sorry to hear it. You know, there are similar difficulties in Italy, but I hadn't realised the problem was so serious in Switzerland.'

I couldn't believe it. A city as international as Geneva… It wasn't the first time I'd heard about this problem and sometimes I was surprised by certain hostile attitudes towards foreigners. I decided to read up in the subject, and I found a United Nations report on precisely this issue. The UN special reporter Doudou Diéne said, and I quote:

'Racism, discrimination and xenophobia are present in Switzerland. There is an almost total absence of means of complaint for victims. Swiss law contains principles which make it possible to fight racism but there is no ad hoc national legislation.'

Then, on 26th January, 2005, an article appeared on the local news site (swissinfo.ch); the gist of it was:

'Black people feel unliked in Switzerland. According to an in-depth study by the Commission Against Racism, black people do not consider themselves accepted by society. Various incidents in the course of their daily life confirm that this is indeed the case.'

The Master's course was over and unfortunately we hadn't all passed, in spite of the immense effort we had put in. The minimum pass mark was 4; with 3.9 you failed. Swiss rigour and seriousness are a reality. I was one of the lucky ones to have passed.

We were all really tired out by our efforts and those who hadn't passed were bitterly disappointed. Rachel told me that after all the hard work she would spend the summer relaxing and unwinding in the mountains, where she would go walking with a friend in the most out-of-the-way spots they could find. They would sleep in mountain shelters and be in bed by eight every evening. Rachel was only 26 and at her age I would have gone to Ibiza and had a crazy time getting drunk in the nightclubs and meeting new people. The world is a wonderful place because everyone is so different!

The James Blunt Concert

I was glad that the Master's course was now over. I felt drained, but at the same time I was delighted at not having to follow any more lessons. What a liberation!

We decided to celebrate the end of the course by having dinner in a Mexican restaurant with a group of friends. Harold and I were then going on to a James Blunt concert as an added bonus.

I was very happy about this: I love James Blunt. Apart from the fact that he is drop-dead gorgeous, he has the voice of an angel and I know all his songs off by heart. I love James Blunt. Harold and I were really up for it, excited and ready to go wild.

We arrived at the concert. We didn't have to queue and everything was perfectly orderly. It couldn't have been more different from the chaotic bedlam you get at concerts in Italy. No one shouted too loud and there were no girls screaming hysterically for their idol. There was an air of great calm. It was like being at the theatre or a classical music concert. Or at the premiere of an opera. Everything went perfectly smoothly. And suddenly there was James on the stage, gorgeous, funny and singing divinely. I went wild! Harold and I sang at the top of our voices and danced along with the music. I was having a great time.

I was aware that all around us there was a funereal calm: no one was singing, dancing, or getting excited. Everyone, even the younger people, was listening in silence as James sang. They weren't even tapping their feet! I started wondering whether this country had some law that prohibited singing and dancing during concerts. Surely not...

Now he was singing my favourite song: "You are beautiful." The atmosphere was perfect – the lights, the sound – I was in ecstasy. No one stopped me. I sang along happily at the top of my voice while Harold danced like a dervish. My husband is one of the very few men I have met who love dancing and dance really well. He was sweating like a watermelon at a barbecue but he didn't give a damn; he was having a great time and nothing else mattered. We laughed and took photos of that hunk James!

Suddenly a man came over to me and, to my great surprise, said:

'Can you give the singing a rest – I can't hear the concert and you're disturbing me. And tell your friend to stop dancing. He's already elbowed me in the stomach.'

I couldn't help it: I burst out laughing. I decided to ignore him and we carried on singing and dancing. What was the guy going to do? Call the police?

We had a fantastic time, not only because the concert was brilliant but also because it was so surprising to see an audience so quiet and self-controlled. For us it really was a new experience.

Work

I Found a Job!

After all the stress of the University, I took a well-deserved holiday with my family in Puglia. In September I returned to Geneva happy because I HAD FOUND A JOB!

The Master's degree played a key role in this; it really did help me. One of the banks that had sponsored the course offered me a training contract for a year.

I was 35 and had seven years professional experience, and here I was doing an internship. It had been made clear to me during the various interviews I had had, that work experience outside Switzerland counted for nothing. For them it was as if I had never worked. To be honest I don't know why. Perhaps they think that beyond the Swiss borders lies a world of card-carrying layabouts and idlers. Or maybe they're just prejudiced against Italians. In any case, I had no choice. I had to accept the training contract. One of the teachers from the Master's course, a woman I admired enormously, reassured me:

'Sometimes you need to take a step backwards so that you can then take a big step forwards.'

Maybe. But to me it feels like I've walked a long way back just in the hope of being able to take one step forward.

I began working in mid-September. The Ecole Internationale le Mignon started on the 1st of September, so I had time to get to know Alice's and Dante's teachers. One day when I picked Alice up from school she was particularly happy and enthusiastic. As soon as she saw me she ran to me and threw her arms around me. It's so great being a mother!

We said goodbye to her new teacher, Erika, and headed for the car. I asked her:

'Are your new classmates nice? Did you play? Did you have a good time?'

'Yes, Mummy, I played with my new friend all day. Screw you.'

'Sorry, Alice, what was that? You played with who?'

Irritated by the question – and also because she does not like having to repeat herself – Alice raised her voice:

'Screw you! I told you: screw you.'

Just at that moment we ran into one of the *VIP mothers*, Elisabetta. She is from one of the wealthiest and most noble families in Milan. Elisabetta is the kind of person for who even a word like "crétin" is far too vulgar for her to even think about using. She is beautiful, very chic and looks like Carla Bruni. She made no attempt to disguise her shock at hearing a little girl say such things. Embarrassed at the thought of what Elisabetta must be thinking, I lost my temper with Alice:

'Are you crazy? What has got into you? You're only three; you can't use words like that. Who taught you to say that? I send you to one of the most expensive international schools in the world and you bring language like this home! Don't you ever say that again!'

Alice looked at me in astonishment:

'Why are you shouting at me? I don't understand why you are so angry with me; I haven't done anything to you.'

The next day I took Alice to school and, with some embarrassment, asked the teacher if there was a child in the class whose name was something like Scru...

'Well, there's a new girl just arrived from Kenya: Skruyu. That little black girl with the red dress and the pigtails over there. Her grandfather is the Kenyan ambassador in Geneva. Her parents stayed in Africa and she has come to live here with her grandparents.'

So that was the answer to the mystery: Skruyu, a sweet little girl whose eyes lit up when Alice came into the classroom. She ran around happily with the other children but there was a certain sadness in her face. It seemed crazy to me that she was living with her grandparents. She was only three. Had her parents abandoned her? I liked her immediately and felt very guilty for shouting at Alice.

One could only hope that Skruyu's grandparents would come up with a nickname for the child that would save her from a hellish future in school!

Back outside, in the school car park, I ran into Ana, one of the *Mothers Who Just Happen to Be Here*. She had moved to Geneva from Seville just a few months earlier on account of her husband's job. Friendly, funny and lively, she had a real ability to crack me up. She was a typical southern Spanish lady, who had much in common with us southern Italian women. If I want to have a girls' night out, I always invite her because I know we'll have a laugh. Ana has three beautiful, lively children. She came up to me and sighed:

'I need to talk to you. Have you got five minutes for a coffee?'

'Of course, no problem. You look out of sorts. Is everything okay?'

'I am in a state of shock. I'm feeling very wound-up and to be honest I still can't believe it. Yesterday my husband's company organised a welcome seminar for the newly arrived wives. They billed it as 'Information on Swiss Culture', so I was expecting things like advice on where to go skiing or which restaurants do the best fondue. I still can't believe...'

I started laughing. The expression of astonishment on Ana's face was too funny for words. She then went on to tell me about a test in which she had got one of the answers "wrong". The guy running the seminar had then had a real go at her... The question was:

'Your best friend is driving and you are in the passenger seat. She hits a man, slightly injuring him. The accident occurs on a road where the speed limit is forty kilometres an hour. Your friend was doing fifty kilometres an hour. The police arrive and ask you what speed your friend was driving at. Do you say forty kilometres an hour or do you tell the truth and report your friend?'

Being a good southern woman, Ana had replied that nothing in the world would bring her to report a friend and that she would have made a false statement to the police. He had replied that it was foreigners like her who ruined the peace and tranquillity of life in Switzerland, and they had a terrible argument. Apparently 97% of Swiss would report their friend in this situation.

I wonder why I wasn't surprised by the way the guy had reacted. I tried to calm Ana and to explain to her that there were big cultural differences between Italy, Spain and Switzerland. In Italy and Spain too, I pointed out, we had plenty of crazy rules and customs, and the Swiss were undoubtedly better organised than we were. And our host country certainly had many positive sides that we shouldn't forget, and in many ways we were lucky to be there.

I listened patiently while Ana complained at length about the treatment she had had to put up with after her two-year-old daughter touched an apple in a supermarket and her five-year-old son broke a glass in a restaurant.

I explained to her that I had been through much the same. Since arriving in this paradise (apparently), I had been reproached hundreds of times simply because my children were behaving like children! Alice moved a bottle of detergent off a shelf in a supermarket and Dante had a pee in the garden of the municipal swimming pool. The swimming pool caretaker was so angry he nearly had a heart attack. My son was so traumatised by the experience that he has never been able to pee outside since.

There are lots of parks with playgrounds here full of greenery and trees. In some ways it's an ideal place to bring up children. You start thinking that it's a country that really cares about kids' wellbeing, and then you are shocked when they won't even let you into a restaurant because your pushchair is too big.

So I tried consoling Ana and advised her to fight back if people treated her like that. It makes you feel much better to stand up to them even if it gets you nowhere. I told her about how two weeks earlier, on the way back from our holidays in Italy, Alice and Dante were playing with the luggage trolley in Geneva airport. A policeman of about sixty zoomed over and said to me exasperatedly:

'Your children are causing a disturbance. They are ill-mannered little savages!'

Enraged, I stared him right in the eyes and retorted:

'There's still plenty of time for my children to learn manners. It's too late for you, though! You're always going to be ill-mannered. You're a lost cause.'

I walked off with my head held high, while Harold stood laughing at the astonished expression on the policeman's face. My friend Ana laughed her head off. She was in a good mood again.

My First Days in the Bank

There were about fifteen lawyers and other legal staff in the legal department of the bank. It was my first day at work. That morning I had woken up very early and had taken great care with my make-up and hair. I was very nervous and excited. I put on one of my favourite dress suits and boarded the train for Lausanne. I was happy to be going back to work. The bank was in the centre of Lausanne. From the station you have quite an uphill walk to reach the enormous building. From door to door it had taken me an hour and ten minutes but that didn't bother me at all. It was a glorious, sunny day and Lausanne is a beautiful city. The people getting off the train and heading for the offices were smartly dressed in suits and ties. I had missed this world of working people running in all directions clutching plastic cups brimful of coffee. I felt a surge of adrenaline as I got near the bank's offices. At last I was feeling active and productive; I was no longer a desperate housewife or a late-graduating student. For a moment I remembered that I was thirty-five and still only a trainee, but the sight of people having breakfast outside the city bars distracted me. I would soon get to know this city and be having lunch in beautiful restaurants in the centre with my new colleagues. A new era was beginning for me.

I arrived at the staff entrance. I rang the bell and the door opened. I went in and, with a smile, gave the doorman my name. He motioned to me to wait and called through to the secretary in the bank's legal department. A few minutes later a cheerful, smiling woman called Maria arrived and introduced herself as the secretary of the manager, Mr Hunziker. Maria asked me to follow her. The bank was enormous, full of people scurrying along its wide corridors. We went through a series of doors, each of which opened automatically after Maria inserted a magnetic card. We took a lift to the fifth floor. She took me into the secretary's office and pointed to my office: a desk hidden behind a bookcase. Maria informed me:

'This is the trainee's office. I'm here for you if you need any information. Mr. Hunziker will see you as soon as he can.'

'Thank you, Maria, you're very kind. As we're in the same office, I'm sure I will take you up on your offer.'

Shortly afterwards, Mr. Jaker approached me. A very kind and good-humoured man, he was in charge of organising my training at the bank. He showed me the legal department's cafeteria, where all the legal staff were enjoying their coffee. One by one, they introduced themselves. They struck me as easy-going, funny and very sociable. There was a very relaxed, informal atmosphere. I sat down and had a cup of tea with them. I felt at ease and had the impression my colleagues all got on very well with each other.

A few minutes later Mr. Hunziker, the manager of the legal department, came in. Everyone greeted him and he smiled at me:

'Welcome. As soon as you have finished your tea, please come and see me in my office.'

Flustered, I stood and said:

'I have finished. If I'm not disturbing, I will come now.'

I followed him into his office and he explained to me what my job would involve. We then spoke about my family and the reasons why I was in Switzerland. I felt I was getting on well with my new boss and that I would enjoy working for him. I returned to my office and Maria gave me a magnetic card to get into the bank. I would have to clock in and clock out, and I would work eight hours and twenty-four minutes every day. Maria told me:

'Never forget your magnetic card; otherwise there is no way of calculating how many hours you have worked, and the bank's security people won't let you in.'

I smiled and replied:

'Don't worry, there's no way I'll forget it. Look, I'll put it in my wallet now.'

The next day I left my wallet, with the magnetic card in it, at home. When I arrived at the bank and realised I had forgotten it, I decided to try my charm on the security man. Maria was doubtless exaggerating; he was bound to let me in! I smiled at him and said:

'Good morning! You know, this morning I was really busy what with one thing and another... I live in Geneva, you see, and it takes me an hour and ten minutes to get to work. I had to drop the children off at school – they're still really small – and it was one of those terrible mornings...I don't know if you have children yourself and can understand what I'm saying, but...well, the thing is, I don't know how it happened but I've forgotten my magnetic card, the one for getting into the bank. Could you let me in anyway?'

Without even looking at me, he brusquely replied:

'No.'

I was aware that flexibility was not a strong point in this country but I wasn't going to give up so easily:

'I really must get into the bank. Can we find a solution?'

'Let's see if your boss will give me authorisation. How long have you been working in the bank?'

'Only since yesterday. This is my second day at work.'

'Can you show me some proof of identity?'

Instinctively, I began rooting in my bag but then remembered that I didn't have my wallet or any of my documents with me:

'Unfortunately my documents are in the wallet which I have left at home. I'm sorry.'

'How can I be sure that you're telling me the truth? If you give me your name and surname I have no way of checking that you are that person. Give me your boss's name, please.'

'Certainly. Mr. Hunziker, director of the legal department. He's my boss.'

The man tried to call the director but got no answer. He must have tried at least ten times. Then I recalled:

'Sorry, I just remembered that Mr Hunziker is on holiday for a week starting from today.'

'Then give me the name of one your colleagues.'

'Maria or Sandrine. But... their surnames... yes, the secretary is called Maria. I'm sorry, but I don't know her surname and I don't know the surnames of my other colleagues. As I told you, I only started working here yesterday.'

'Madame, do you realise that there are two thousand people working in this bank? How do you expect me to find Maria? Do you have any idea how many Marias must work in this bank?'

After a long search and various telephone calls, he told me that Maria was coming to get me. She arrived laughing and assured the security guard that I was indeed the trainee. Then she consoled me:

'Don't worry. The same thing happened to me after I had been working here for twenty-two years. They didn't want to let me in. It's normal practice. They're just very strict in their checks.'

I liked Maria. She was always smiling and it was good sharing an office with her. Then I found out that she was from Malaga, Spain, and I liked her even more. I have lots of friends in Malaga and the first time I went there I felt like I was in Bari. They have the same easy-going attitude as the southern Italians and a real love for life. I felt at home straight away.

With Maria I often ended up talking about Spain and her family. She was born in Lausanne to Spanish parents. Her parents then went back to Malaga to enjoy their Swiss pensions. She married a Spanish guy, had two children, but had never lived in Malaga. She often went back to see her family in Spain, but her life was in Lausanne.

Every morning, with some considerable difficulty, I woke up at 6:30 a.m. At 7:20 I caught the train and at 8:30 I was in the office. It was a struggle for me to get up that early. I felt like I was arriving very early at the office, but a lot of my colleagues had already been there a good while by the time I got there. Maria got up every morning at 5:30, had breakfast with her children about 6:00 and arrived at the office at 7:00. It seemed to me like a hellish way of living, having to cope with such anti-social times. But she wasn't the only one. There were lots of people getting up very early in the morning. The pace of their life was very different from what I had been used to in Bari!

The Ticket Inspector

The weeks were passing quickly and my job was becoming more and more interesting. I was writing contracts for deals with foreign banks. One morning about eleven I received a telephone call from Dante's school.

Maria answered the telephone:

'Flo, there's a phone call for you. It's your son's school.'

My heart started thumping like crazy; I was in a panic, thinking there must have been an accident. My mind started turning horrible thoughts around. Dante must be hurt, or maybe they had lost him…

My greatest fear is that my children will get lost. I don't trust anyone to look after them properly. I'm always convinced that other people won't be careful enough. In Dante's class there are fifteen children, two teachers and countless other staff: those who work in the car park, those who help the children cross the road, plain clothes security men, bodyguards – in all there must be about thirty people! And yet I never feel completely at ease about leaving the children at school.

I picked up the phone and, with trembling hand, stammered:

'Yes, this is Dante's mother; what has happened?'

'Madame, don't worry, nothing has happened to your children.'

They know me; they know all too well that I'm a paranoid lunatic. I got them to explain several times that the climbing frames in the playground were not dangerous at all. I always accompany them on school trips or else I persuade Harold to go with them. I'm forever checking in the classroom that there aren't any dangerous new toys and I hassle the poor teachers – who have the patience of saints – to remind my children to put on their hats, scarves and jackets when they go out to play.

'Dante has a bit of a temperature and has vomited. Could you come and get him?'

'I'm on my way. I'm at work in Lausanne but I'll jump on the next train and be with you as soon as I can.'

I grabbed my jacket, hastily told Maria I was leaving and ran to the train station like a woman possessed. I couldn't stop thinking about poor, sick Dante waiting for me. There was a train leaving in a few minutes and I just had to be on it! It was a race against the clock. The train was leaving in exactly 12 minutes, and I couldn't afford to miss it. And of course the damned trains were always so unbelievably punctual.

At the speed of an Olympic sprinter in the 100 metres final, I legged it towards the station. I checked which platform the train was leaving from and nearly killed myself running up the steps in my heels; wearing seven-centimetre heels means you risk falling from a dangerous height. Somehow I survived the steps but I was starting to hate my shoes – for the sake of looking good in the office I had put my life at risk. Out of breath and with my heart racing, I reached the platform. The train was still there!

I pushed the button to open the doors to the carriage. The doors opened but before I could jump on they closed again. The ticket inspector, who was already on the train, closed them to stop me getting on.

I screamed:

'Let me on! I have to get to my son! He's sick!'

I pressed the button again and the doors opened. I was actually on the train now… but with great force – this couldn't really be happening! – the ticket inspector pushed me off again, and before closing the doors, snapped:

'Next time, don't be late! You've delayed our departure.'

I was so out of breath I couldn't speak. In fact my lungs were screaming so hard for oxygen that I thought I was going to have a heart attack. The train pulled out and I stood there with my finger still poised to press the button to open the doors.

I wasn't late, Mr. Ticket Inspector, I was on time. And human beings are more important than your petty, pointless rules. Have you ever heard the words "humanity", "understanding", "tolerance" or "solidarity", Mr. Ticket Inspector? All you care about is whether your train leaves on time, and nothing else matters. Who cares if the train leaves one second late? My son is sick.

I stood there unable to move, pathetically watching the train disappear into the distance as if it were my last hope of survival. The next train was in thirty minutes, an eternity when you have a sick child waiting for you. I was sad, inexpressibly sad. I felt like crying. I looked at the faces of the people around me in the station, searching for an answer. There was a shop at the end of the platform where a child with his mother was eating an ice cream. I bought Dante a little gift to ease my sense of guilt at being a working mother.

Sandrine

The months passed and my enthusiasm for work was undiminished. The work was always interesting and my career at the bank was moving full sail ahead. In the coffee breaks I would chat away happily with my colleagues and we soon got to know about what was happening in each other's lives. I got on really well with all my colleagues, but especially with Maria and Sandrine.

At only 25, Sandrine was the youngest lawyer in the legal department; she was a lovely girl, very kind and always willing to help. A perfectionist, she worked hard and was good at her job. Every day she would get to pass on files to me and we would end up working together. I was more than happy to have lunch with her and Maria. They were both really easy-going, and we could talk about anything, be it work, colleagues or our personal lives. My colleagues seemed satisfied with my work and my boss quickly realised that my previous experience was extremely useful in my present job.

After I had been there for six months, Mr. Hunziker offered me a proper contract with the bank and the opportunity to move up from my rather sad position as a 35-year-old trainee. I was enthusiastic at the prospect and particularly happy that my previous years of work were no longer looking like wasted time. They offered me a contract as a legal adviser, which is one step up from the first rung on the career ladder for a legal expert in a bank. And so I became a fully-integrated employee of the bank.

The fantastic thing about my new contract was that it allowed me the chance to work part-time. For the first few months I continued to work full-time and then asked my boss if I could switch to part-time. The Swiss labour market thus put me in the marvellous position of being able to work without any sense of guilt. I worked three days a week and was well-paid. A twenty-one hour working week – fantastic! The other two days a week I was with my children. All the lawyer mothers in the legal department worked part-time. The great thing about my contract was that I had an interesting, high-level job and I could do it part time. That is something very rare, even in Switzerland. My boss was a splendid family man with children of his own, which made him sensitive to the needs of a working mother like me. What more could you ask for?

When I first found out about the contract, I was beside myself with joy. I announced the news to Sandrine. Sandrine congratulated me on my promotion but a few minutes later, as I was walking down the corridor, I heard someone crying desperately in one of the offices. I had no idea what was going on and thought that maybe someone had had news of some family tragedy. Rather worried, I went to ask the secretaries what had happened. It turned out it was Sandrine crying because of my contract. Apparently, she didn't think I deserved to be promoted to the level above hers. Although I tried to smooth things over, Sandrine simply stopped talking to me. Our friendship was over for good. It had lasted six months.

Maria

Fortunately, I still had Maria, with whom I got on splendidly. We often spoke in Spanish. She was always in a good mood. One day I needed a doctor and Maria advised me to go to hers because he was near the bank. She explained to me that bank regulations allowed employees a maximum of two hours leave for a medical appointment. A week later I left work two hours early to go to the doctor and I let Maria know about it. She smiled and said goodbye. The appointment lasted one and a half hours. Afterwards I went straight home without going back to the bank.

The following day, as soon as I arrived at work, my boss called me into his office because he wanted to talk to me. This was a meeting which would forever change how I felt about my job.

I went into his office, which overlooked Lake Léman. I remember the water was a magnificent shade of blue. I felt calm and at ease. From the very first day I had enjoyed working for my boss. He was an intelligent guy of about fifty, who really knew his stuff and was good at his job. A man who could never be defined as ordinary. He looked me straight in the eye and said:

'I have been told that yesterday you went to the doctor's and then made out that the appointment lasted two hours, when in fact it appears that the appointment did not last that long and that you have made a false statement. In addition, I have received a series of complaints from your colleagues concerning various episodes of misconduct on your part, such as, for example, your time of arrival in the office and similar things. Some of your colleagues are extremely jealous of you and maintain that I give you preferential treatment. Don't worry. I know you are good at your job and I don't give any weight to this kind of criticism. However, do be careful and do try to avoid such things happening in the future.'

I sat there in front of my boss with my gormless expression on my face. I was lost for words, dumbstruck. It was beyond belief and I was in a state of shock. Had Maria, my friend from Malaga, reported me? Or one of my other colleagues. How was this possible? I had never had an inkling they might be jealous or envious of me. I was utterly confused. What were they jealous of? I thanked my boss and left his office without saying another word. I didn't feel well at all: I could hardly breathe. I needed to talk to someone about how frustrated, astonished and disappointed I felt. I couldn't take it all in. I was suddenly left with no one I could trust. I felt betrayed. My friendship with Maria had lasted seven months.

I had a think and decided to speak to Jeraldine. I was sure she had nothing to do with any of this. I had got on straight away with Jeraldine. She was an attractive, sweet-natured woman with four children. Originally from the German part of Switzerland, she was tall, slim and blond, with smiling blue eyes. She was highly intelligent. I told her what had happened. She wasn't in the least surprised, and sympathised:

'I know what you mean. I've had to put up with the same kind of treatment for years. Don't even waste time thinking about it. Just act as if nothing has happened. You can't change your colleagues. I've been working in this bank for seven years and I've been through the same thing more times than I can remember. It doesn't surprise me any more; it doesn't even upset me.'

It was reassuring to be able to talk to Jeraldine, and from that day on she was my only true friend in the office.

Eight months later, Jeraldine was promoted to a managerial role and became my boss. I was delighted for her and congratulated her warmly. Jeraldine is an extraordinary woman: a sensitive, caring mother and highly professional in her job. During the departmental meeting – at which everyone was present - Mr. Hunziker announced the good news about Jeraldine's promotion. Nobody congratulated her; in fact the silence was so overwhelming, you'd have thought someone had died.

My boss informed me that I'd be moving to a new office. I was no longer a trainee and would now be sharing an office with Fréderic. I was pleased. This was good news. The new office was extremely spacious and had a breathtaking view over Lake Léman

Fréderic was the same age as me. He struck me as easy-going and sociable. Maybe we could even become friends – God knows, I needed friends in that place. But from the first day I moved into his office, Fréderic and I never really talked very much. One day I asked him:

'Do you fancy having lunch together?'

'No, I'd prefer to read the newspaper.'

I worked with him for two years. Our desks were barely a metre apart and I knew nothing about him, his family, his life, his hobbies… absolutely nothing. Fréderic was a fervent believer in the idea that one's professional and personal lives should be kept separate. Colleagues are colleagues and nothing more. I understood that, but it wasn't like I was aiming to become his best friend, only confidant, soul-mate and mother of his children! It just would have been nice to have the occasional light-hearted chat between colleagues. Was that asking too much? If I remember correctly, Fréderic and I spoke together on precisely two occasions – for a total of seven minutes each time – on subjects not directly related to work.

Long Chat Number 1: I was ill, had lost my voice, was coughing like a horse that smoked, and could feel a temperature coming on. Fréderic looked at me:

'Go home; you're not well. You can finish the contract another day. Do you realise you can't even talk?'

He repeated this at least ten times over the next twenty minutes. I was almost moved to tears at the thought of his concern for me, at this unexpected solicitude!

Suddenly he flung open the office windows. Outside it was at least minus five, and I could see myself dying in no time. I asked him:

'Please close the window; I'll catch a chill.'

I could see he was getting anxious, overwrought. He kept looking at me, and finally said:

'You've got to go now. I'm catching your flu. I'm starting to get a sore throat.'

I laughed and said:

'I'll be gone soon. And, anyway, don't be ridiculous: you can't catch a bad cold in just a few minutes – it takes days.'

He got more and more annoyed and worked up. After a while he went out. He was gone a few minutes, and when he came back he was carrying a small package. He opened it, took out a green mask, like one of those that surgeons use during an operation, and put it on. Then he opened a bottle of tablets and took some vitamins. He kept looking at me in annoyance. I kept looking at him and laughing. He didn't see the funny side of it, and irritably asked me to stop. That was the day I had most fun with my colleague Fréderic.

Long Chat Number 2: Like the rest of my colleagues, I received a bonus with my salary. The amount we got was confidential information. Fréderic was not happy with his bonus and, although no one gets to know how much anyone else is given, he wanted to know about mine. I had no intention of telling him, but he kept skirting round the subject, coming up with strange and pointless questions, without ever asking me straight out. Jokingly, I said:

'I got a fantastic bonus this year! I'm thinking of buying a villa on the lake in the centre of Lausanne.'

He didn't find it funny!

Death

My colleague Matthieu was always in a good mood, always cheerful and smiling. Our relationship was hardly deep, but we got on well. He struck me as being a good guy, the kind of person who will always help you out. We would often run into each other in the room where the printer was, and we'd chat happily about this and that. I noticed that for a few days Matthieu had seemed very down and less sociable than usual. I went into his office and breezily asked: 'Is everything okay? You look sad. Is something wrong?'

Matthieu looked me in the eye and then looked away towards the window. It was a cold, wet spring day. He looked at me again and, with tears in his eyes, replied:

'Thank you for asking. It's good to know that you care about how I feel. No one else in this office does. I'm devastated. One of my fourteen-year-old son's close friends committed suicide yesterday.'

His voice shook as he told me about the tragedy. I wanted to give him a hug, but in Switzerland there is an unwritten rule that you don't show affection in the workplace.

'A fourteen-year-old boy, but that's crazy! It's incredible. I can't believe it! How can someone so young... still a teenager...? What happened?'

'I don't know, but he's the second kid in the school to kill himself. It's a small school, a tragedy for all of us.'

I felt dreadfully sorry for Matthieu. It must be a terribly painful experience, especially for his son. I was absolutely gobsmacked. At my secondary school in Bari there were about two thousand teenagers, but no one ever committed suicide. I went back to my office and carried on working but, I couldn't stop thinking about this terrible, tragic affair. When I got home I talked to Harold about it, and like me he had never heard of anyone from his school – in Amsterdam – committing suicide. Then, being a natural mathematician, he pointed out that two suicides in one school were statistically very high.

It was disturbing. I wanted to get a clearer idea of what was going on, so I read up on the subject. I found a press release from 10 November, 2008 on the official site of the canton of Vaud about a new mental initiative set up by the health department. The document was published on the official site of the canton of Vaud (www.santepublique.vd.ch) and the figures it contained seriously shocked me. The main conclusions of in-depth research by a group of qualified Swiss psychiatrists were:

- One in two Swiss suffer, at some point in their lives, from psychological problems that require medical treatment;
- In the canton of Vaud alone, there are an estimated 120 suicides a year;
- In Switzerland, about 25% of children and adolescents suffer from psychological problems; in the rest of Europe, according to a study by the World Health Organisation, the proportion of children and adolescents suffering from psychological problems is around 12%;
- In Switzerland, suicide is the main cause of death amongst young people aged between 15 and 34. According to the World Health Organisation, this is well above the world average;
- 1,284 people committed suicide in 2004. That is equivalent to 21 out of every 100,000 men, and more than 9 out of every 100,000 women;
- Switzerland has by far the highest number of attempted suicides in Europe – the estimated average is about 10,000 per year;
- Interviews with 567 adolescents (aged between 11 and 16) revealed that 13% have suffered from serious depression;
- Suicide is even more widespread amongst the elderly. The rate for those over 70 is 40 per 100,000. For people over 75 years of age, the rate is 85% higher.

While I was in lost in these unhappy thoughts more sad news arrived the same day. My mother called me to inform me that my grandmother, Clementina, had died. She was 86 and for years had been suffering from Alzheimer's disease, but I was devastated by the news. I knew that she had not been well for a long time, and that her age and physical condition had not given grounds for optimism, but when I heard the news I burst into tears. I had always had a special relationship with my wonderful grandparents, so even though my grandmother hadn't been able to recognise me for at least a decade and conversation had been impossible, her death still came as a great shock.

It's at times like those that you realise just how far away you live from your family. I couldn't work, and tearfully asked for leave to go home. Sobbing, I explained what had happened and that I wanted to book a flight and depart immediately for Bari.
'My grandmother has died. I want to try and make it to the funeral.'
One of the secretaries replied coldly:
'Regulations state that you may only leave the office in the event of the death of your spouse, children, parents or immediate family. Other relatives don't count; therefore you have no right to leave.'
Sandrine was sitting next to the secretary munching a roll. She stared at me so icily I could feel the air freezing around her, and nodded to confirm that the secretary was right; she didn't stop chewing.
I left anyway without bothering to argue. As usual, the regulations were considered more important than any human feelings.

The 5 Commandments

The whole problem of tense relationships between colleagues in the legal department finally blew up. The bank asked us to fill in anonymous questionnaires about what we were dissatisfied with in the office. The result was disastrous.

The unfortunate head of the department, Mr. Hunziker, who had been counting on the common sense and goodwill of the employees, had to rethink his strategy. Some colleagues pressured the poor guy into drawing up a handbook containing a code of behaviour for the workplace. The new rules had absolutely nothing to do with the work itself, but concerned how workers should behave towards their colleagues. Rather as if, when we were kids, someone had given out a handbook with rules on how to behave with your friends and acquaintances, along the lines of: don't kiss strangers with your tongue; don't take part in riots; don't laugh if you have parsley stuck between your teeth; don't swear; don't fart in the presence of other human beings, etc.

It was an absurd situation. I had to read the Five Commandments about twenty times because I simply couldn't believe that such a thing was possible in a normal workplace. Why would fifteen serious professional people need a list of written rules in order to be able to maintain a civilised working relationship? It was astounding... During a meeting of the whole legal department, Mr. Hunziker gave out a new version of the Five Commandments for a workplace. These were to be followed so as to restore order, tranquillity and a good atmosphere amongst colleagues. I hardly need point out that the plan didn't work.

The new rules were:

- everyone is to ensure that his/her behaviour and subjects of conversation in no way hurt or denigrate any colleague;
- the guiding principle is that everyone should take care of his/her own business and not intrude on that of his/her colleagues;

153

- if any worker feels he/she is being unequally or unfairly treated or is the object of the jealousy or envy of colleagues he/she should immediately communicate the problem to his/her superior;
- colleagues with a small workload must not delegate files to busier colleagues;
- any worker who is the object of offensive remarks or who has the impression he/she is ill-thought of by his/her colleagues should discuss the matter with his/her superior.

My Brother's Wedding

I had been working in the bank for a year when my brother Michele telephoned me and said:
'We've fixed a date; we're getting married on December 7th.'

My brother had been stuck at the age of twenty for a good twenty years. Finally, at nearly forty he had taken the big decision to settle down. He was one of the hard-core Baresi who, even as forty approaches, continue to live as if they were in their 20s. I was to be his witness at the wedding and I wanted to get to Bari a few days beforehand to help out my mother, who was on the verge of a nervous breakdown trying to organise everything.

Harold and I both took a week off work, and I trailed all around Geneva looking for a dress for the big day. I also started training my children for their job as ring-bearers. At last we were all set: we had our plane tickets, my children and I had our new outfits, and in five days we would be heading south.

Harold, being the Nordic member of the family, wondered:
'Do we have to get authorisation from Dante's teacher for the week of school he will miss?'
'Come off it, he's only six! Don't be ridiculous!'
'We *are* living in Switzerland, don't forget. I'll have a word with his teacher tomorrow.'

The following day, while I was working with a colleague on the details of a contract, I got a call from Harold:
'Dante's teacher told me that we have to make a written request to the headmaster asking for five days holiday. She gave me the impression there is no guarantee that we'll get permission.'
'Are you joking? This is my brother's wedding! Are they out of their minds? Don't worry. When I tell them it's because my brother's getting married they'll understand, you'll see... what with it being a family matter and all... I'll write to the headmaster myself today.'

A few days later we received a reply from the headmaster. It read:

'The school cannot authorise Dante to miss five days of school. According to federal law, Dante's absence in such circumstances could not be considered justifiable. Moreover, his absence would set an extremely bad example to his classmates. If Dante should fail to attend school on those days, we shall hold you responsible.'

The last sentence had a threatening tone. We were well aware that the school had no qualms about failing children as young as six. And it was a particularly difficult year for Dante. He was in the Francophone section of the school, which was based on the model of the French lycée. Or in other words, you studied like crazy from 6 to 18-years-old. You ruined your childhood and adolescence by working yourself to death, and then you were Mr. Cool for the rest of your life because you had been to a French lycée.

I didn't know if I was going to leave my son in a school where six-year-olds read poetry books and did multiplications. I didn't know what kind of academic future lay ahead of him. But I did know, without a shadow of doubt, that if they failed him, then I might be capable of slashing all four tyres on the headmaster's car. And if I found out that his teacher was to blame in any way, I would make a scene in front of the *VIP Mothers* and *Mothers from Diplomatic Families*. I didn't have time to waste worrying about this ridiculous letter, and the following day we set off happily for Bari.

On our return I decided to contact the headmaster and speak to him in person about the letter. I met him in his office and he said to me: 'Madame, Swiss law only allows a child to be absent from school for health reasons, which must be supported by a medical certificate. In other cases, one has to obtain the headmaster's consent, but this is very rarely given. I am obliged, even if this is an international school, to conform to the laws of the country in which the school is located. However, don't worry; we are flexible in this school, and therefore you will not be fined.'

Fined? That's right: parents who step out of line here get fined. Swiss federal law requires children to attend school from the age of six, and any unjustified absence by a pupil is punished. In short, from the day your child turns six, you are stuck in Switzerland during the school year. The headmaster reports those unjustified absences to the Prefect of Police. The Prefect imposes a fine of up to two thousand Swiss francs. The school also keeps a record of lateness on the part of students. The headmaster can report latecomers to the Prefect, who again fines the parents. Incredible, I know, but true.

It's a good job that Italian schools aren't run in the same way; otherwise I would have reduced my parents to abject poverty: I was always late! I was lucky as the school caretaker, with whom I was very good friends, always waited till I was inside before closing the main gate.

My brother's wedding was not considered a just cause for absenting my child from school, but sickness backed up by a medical certificate would have been acceptable. No doctor in Switzerland, of course, would ever falsify a certificate.

My Last Day at Work

After I'd been working for a year and a half at the bank, life in the office had become very lonely. My relations with my colleagues, which were already far from idyllic, deteriorated seriously after I asked my boss for a month's unpaid leave. This had to do with my Master's degree, as after one year of work I had to write a thesis in order to get the Diploma from the University of Geneva. Being an understanding man, my boss granted my request. This led to me being seen as a favourite who was taking advantage of her boss' generosity.

I had had the temerity to make requests and was enjoying privileges that no one else in the bank had dreamt of asking for in the last twenty years. Or rather, that no one had had the guts to ask for. When I got back to the office, literally no one would speak to me, except my friend Jeraldine. I always ended up eating alone if she wasn't around. Her office was the only place in the bank where I felt really at ease. I myself had no wish to make the effort to speak to the other people; I was tired of the whole situation, and disgusted with the way so many colleagues kept reporting each other to their respective superiors.

There were now two quite different Flo's: the normal, lively, sociable, easy-going, good-humoured, smiling version, who had lots of friends; and the office version, who was sad, lonely, distrustful and anti-social.

I felt trapped. I was suffering from some kind of "office sickness". It was no fun getting up at six, rushing to catch two different trains and often missing one, or eating alone in the office cafeteria – the alternative was clocking out and getting behind with the required number of working hours. In 18 months I had eaten in a Lausanne restaurant only twice. More than anything else, I was tired of hearing people say things like:

- 'Of course, you went to university in Italy, where it's much easier...'

- 'Very Italian, the way you type on the computer with just two fingers…'
- 'It must be nice to have such long holidays; in twenty years I've never taken more than two weeks at a time…'
- 'How can you stand going back to a country where there's rubbish everywhere?'
- 'Italy's just a mad-house: I could never live there…'
- 'Oh, you're actually working today? So you're not always on holiday…'

There is only so much a human being can take. The job was interesting and my bosses were fantastic, but unfortunately that was not enough to make me happy in my work. I was the only person in my office that hadn't been living in Switzerland for more than twenty years. I was the only real foreigner in the department. I spoke frankly with Jeraldine and we decided that at the end of my contract I would leave the bank.

Finally, my last day at work arrived. I had been at the bank for two years and now had excellent references to help me find a new job. The unemployment rate was so low that I wasn't concerned about my prospects. What was important was that I now had work experience in Switzerland and references from a Swiss employer, the prerequisites for even being considered for any job.

At the end of the working day, I said goodbye to my colleagues and used my magnetic card for the last time. I handed it in to the security man and signed the paper he gave me. I was free at last! What a wonderful feeling of liberation! I went down the steps, the long steps that make Lausanne a special place, the ones I'd walked down every day to the station to catch the train back to Geneva. I didn't rush; I took it one step at a time. I felt relaxed and as if a weight had been taken off me. I stopped halfway down the steps and looked back up at my "prison".

The bank building was very beautiful; I'd never really looked at it properly. It was majestic and enormous. I watched the people making their way to the station. The Geneva train was already in. I went down and got on, smiling to myself. This was the last time I would be making this long journey home. Except this time it didn't seem long: the time flew by. I was happy. I felt as if I'd been freed from a burden, as if I'd just given birth to twins.

Big News

Dinner was almost ready, and Harold had just returned from work. I was cooking and trying to get Dante to finish his homework. We'd nicknamed him "Tortoise", for obvious reasons. When we sat down, Harold helped me serve the children, and then looked at me:
'I had a long chat with my boss today. They've offered me an interesting job in California, in San Diego, for a couple of years. What do you reckon? Do you think you'd be up for it?'
I spluttered out the water I had been drinking.
Dante asked:
'Is California in Italy?'
Such are the advantages of sending your son to an international school… We all burst out laughing, even Alice, who didn't know why.
I was struggling for air. In California it was nearly two hundred years now that they'd been expecting the "Big One", the earthquake that would kill thousands and trigger the biggest tsunami of all time. Experts reckon that the tremor could be so powerful as to slice California off from the rest of the United States. I was imagining the two years there would mean risking our lives. I didn't say anything for a few moments, and then I looked at Harold and smiled:
'Sure. When do we leave?'

Survival Guide for Foreigners in Switzerland

This portion of this book is intended for foreigners who have just arrived in Switzerland. Remember that certain citizens of the Swiss Confederation can get along very happily without you. They are not waiting with open arms to welcome noisy, troublesome foreigners into their midst. You are invading their territory and will be tolerated (just about) only if you don't cause these people any bother or draw attention to yourself.

Remember, too, that some people here are not highly skilled at minding their own business and will devote themselves with great energy and enthusiasm to minding yours. To avoid unpleasantness, tongue-lashings, impromptu verbal attacks and being reported to <u>the</u> police, carefully follow the advice given below:

1)   There are rules for everything. Find out what these rules are and obey them, even if they appear stupid and trivial.

2)   Don't make noise at home. Don't raise your voice, don't have too many parties and don't invite noisy friends to the ones you do have.

3)   Don't mow your lawn on Sundays or after-hours.

4)   Beware of neighbours: they may turn into your worst nightmare. They don't always communicate directly, but via letters, the concierge of your building, or via the police; alternatively they may simply report you to the local council.

5)   Punctuality is obligatory. Always.

6)   When you cross the road using a pedestrian crossing, thank the driver of the car which has stopped to let you pass, by raising your right hand and smiling.

7)   When you pass through customs from France to Switzerland, roll down your window, slow down and courteously greet the "douanier" with a smile. Avoid arguments. Those who live or work across the border are not popular.

8)   Remember that in the eyes of the Swiss you are living in the best-organised, most efficient place on earth: a genuine paradise. Comport yourself correctly; behave accordingly. Don't question their convictions.

9)   Bring up your children carefully. If you are feeling courageous, take them out to eat in a restaurant, but ensure that they do not cause any disturbance. Wherever you take them, do not allow them to disturb the public peace. Even in playgrounds do not allow them to shout or get overexcited, as they may disturb passers-by.

10)   When you park your car, ensure that the vehicle is wholly and precisely within the space delineated by the white lines. Casual parking is strictly prohibited.

11)   Always respect the speed limits. There are speed cameras hidden everywhere.

12)   When travelling by train, never sing with your children, make noise or speak loud on your mobile phone. Trains leave on time and there is no point in risking a heart attack to catch one. If you're late, the train will have left. Don't rush.

13)   Take great care when separating your waste, as mistakes are not tolerated. If you inadvertently throw an old envelope bearing your name and address into the plastic bottles receptacle, you will be in trouble. They will track you down and within days you will receive a threatening letter from the court.

14)   BEWARE!! In certain apartment blocks, regulations forbid the flushing of toilets between the hours of 10 p.m. and 6:30 a.m. In order to avoid arguments with family and neighbours, it is therefore advisable to confine attacks of dysentery to the hours of daylight.

15)   It is essential to study in detail the police regulations for the municipality in which you live. In certain municipalities these local laws are so bizarre that no foreigner of average intelligence could ever imagine they existed. Here are some of the most extreme ones from places around Switzerland:

- It is forbidden to throw snowballs or confetti, or to leave kites in the street.

- It is forbidden to wash malodorous objects or a car with the water from public taps.

- Dust and dirt must not be thrown into the street. Avoid making too much dust when sweeping.

- Noisy dogs that disturb the public must be prevented from doing so. In the event of any such disturbance, the offending animal will be removed to a dog pound, at the owner's expense.

- Aimless riding around, or riding back and forth, on scooters is forbidden in the streets of the municipality. Revving scooter engines is forbidden. (No Italian teenager would be able to survive such prohibitions.)

- Stones gathered in the open countryside may not be placed in the canals or ditches or on the boundaries that divide two properties.

- All actions and forms of behaviour that disturb the public peace and public order are prohibited and punishable by law – in particular: quarrelling, nervous attacks, arguments, gunshots, songs and noisy games, noisy group activities, and excessive car horns or scooter noise.

- In the streets of the municipality it is forbidden to: repair automobiles, climb on trees, posts, gates and lamps of the town hall.

- It is the responsibility of the driver of any vehicle with tyres soiled by contact with mud from a trench or building site to clean those tyres and any stretch of roadway thereby soiled.

- It is forbidden to fire bazookas or cannons (just out of curiosity, but who has a bazooka or cannon at home?).

I can truly appreciate the good side of living in Switzerland as well as laugh at my own experiences. Thanks to these episodes I was able to write this book. I hope you get as much enjoyment out of reading this as I have had while composing it!

Flo

Do you have a Paradise (Apparently) story you would like to share?

Please send an e-mail to:

flo.regina@paradiseapparently.com

Or check our website:

www.paradiseapparently.com